ROUTLEDGE LIBRARY EDITIONS: SOCIOLOGY OF RELIGION

Volume 11

RELIGION AND THE FAMILY

RELIGION AND THE FAMILY
Youth and the Gang Instinct

GEOFFREY HOYLAND

LONDON AND NEW YORK

First published in 1945 by George Allen & Unwin Ltd

This edition first published in 2019
by Routledge
2 Park Square, Milton Park, Abingdon, Oxon OX14 4RN

and by Routledge
52 Vanderbilt Avenue, New York, NY 10017

Routledge is an imprint of the Taylor & Francis Group, an informa business

© 1945 George Allen & Unwin Ltd

All rights reserved. No part of this book may be reprinted or reproduced or utilised in any form or by any electronic, mechanical, or other means, now known or hereafter invented, including photocopying and recording, or in any information storage or retrieval system, without permission in writing from the publishers.

Trademark notice: Product or corporate names may be trademarks or registered trademarks, and are used only for identification and explanation without intent to infringe.

British Library Cataloguing in Publication Data
A catalogue record for this book is available from the British Library

ISBN: 978-0-367-02386-7 (Set)
ISBN: 978-0-429-02545-7 (Set) (ebk)
ISBN: 978-0-367-08653-4 (Volume 11) (hbk)
ISBN: 978-0-367-08656-5 (Volume 11) (pbk)
ISBN: 978-0-429-02356-9 (Volume 11) (ebk)

Publisher's Note
The publisher has gone to great lengths to ensure the quality of this reprint but points out that some imperfections in the original copies may be apparent.

Disclaimer
The publisher has made every effort to trace copyright holders and would welcome correspondence from those they have been unable to trace.

Religion and the Family
YOUTH AND THE GANG INSTINCT

GEOFFREY HOYLAND

LONDON
GEORGE ALLEN & UNWIN LTD
MUSEUM STREET

First Published in 1945
All rights reserved

To a true family gang:
A.W.
L.W.
I. W.
M.W.

THIS BOOK IS PRODUCED IN COMPLETE
CONFORMITY WITH THE AUTHORISED
ECONOMY STANDARD

PRINTED IN GREAT BRITAIN
in 10-Point Plantin Type
BY WILLMER BROTHERS & CO. LTD.
BIRKENHEAD

FOREWORD

THIS little book embodies the substance of two series of broadcast talks given in the Home Service programme of the B.B.C. during the autumn of 1944, the first under the title 'The Family Gang' and the second dealing with 'Home, Children, and Religion.' Since both dealt with aspects of the same subject, though they were sponsored by different departments of the B.B.C., it has seemed desirable to combine them in one book. The first series is embodied in Part I and the second in Part II, though both have been so rewritten, amplified and modified that the B.B.C. must certainly be absolved from any shade of responsibility for what appears in these pages.

G.H.

CONTENTS

CHAPTER		PAGE
	Foreword	5
	Introduction	7

PART I

1	Brains: Old and New	11
2	The Primitive Family Gang	17
3	Young Gangsters	26
4	The New Family Gang	35

PART II

5	Primitive Religions and Parents	46
6	Minds and Words	57
7	Stories	66
8	The Art of Story-telling	74
9	The Galilee Charter	83
10	The Gang at Prayer	91

INTRODUCTION

We have heard much talk in recent years about the break-up of family life and the weakening of parental control. There are many reasons for this change, which amounts to little short of a revolution in the social life of the nation compared with the conditions of half a century ago. The enormous increase in the facilities for quick and easy transport, together with the equally great extension of public amusements, such as skating-rinks, dance-halls and cinemas, has been one powerful factor in the change. Moreover the whole attitude of the State towards the children has altered profoundly during the past century; a hundred years ago children were regarded as the property of their parents who were free to do almost anything they liked to their offspring—short of actually murdering them. Now the State has assumed a general guardianship over the young and the parents are relegated to being little more than their temporary trustees. Compulsory legislation has invaded the nursery, insisting on vaccination in infancy and education from the age of five. Milk and the mid-day meal are to be provided by the State at school, relieving the parents from yet another responsibility. Nursery schools, voluntary to-day, may possibly be compulsory tomorrow; few would be bold enough to maintain that the grandmotherly—or rather foster-motherly—activities of the State in regard to the children have yet reached their limit and that still more searching encroachments on parental responsibility may not be in store for us.

It is no part of my desire or purpose to decry—or even to criticise—these activities on the part of the State. All of them are admirable in intention, and many, so far as they have been realised in practice, have proved of great benefit to the children. But they cast, none the less, a somewhat lurid light upon the civilisation of our time and they form an ironical commentary on the paradox of democracy, for this mass of legislation has been devised by Parliament, and Parliament is—at any rate in theory—elected by the people, and the people are, to a considerable extent, the parents! The parents of England are passing votes of no-confidence in themselves; they are abdicating individually in favour of themselves corporately. Alternatively we may regard these reforms as being examples of class-legislation, the careful and able class legislating for the careless or unable. Whichever view we take we cannot but be aware of the irony of the situation.

Along with this change in public policy there has gone, of course, an equally significant change in the attitude of the children themselves towards their elders in the family circle. Emancipation on all fronts is in the air, and the children have reacted, quite unconsciously, to its influence. They no longer regard their parents with the unquestioning awe and deference of the Victorian epoch, they are apt to question their wisdom and rebel against their authority at an earlier age, and they are much more aware of the claims and attractions of the outside world. The parents have contributed to this by a change in their own attitude; they are not so inclined as they were to mount the high horse and lay down the law, there is more real comradeship, give-and-take, and freedom of expression. The parental pedestal, where it has not disappeared altogether, is many feet lower than it used to be. We may sum it all up by saying that the influence of the family upon the children has decreased markedly both in duration and strength; the children escape from it at an earlier age and even while they are subject to it its influence is weaker and more diluted.

If we are satisfied of the general truth of this statement we have next to ask ourselves whether the change is a good one—is it, as the Quakers say, 'in right ordering'? A considerable body of opinion, associated in the main with left-wing political theory, answers unhesitatingly 'yes'. These people trace very many of the ills of bourgeois society to the over-dependence of children upon their parents, emotionally and economically.

In Soviet Russia the family has been far more thoroughly 'liquidated' as a social unit than it has in England; the State assumes direct responsibility for the children soon after they are born, and the system under which married women are encouraged and expected to pursue independent wage-earning careers inevitably limits home-life, as we in the West understand the phrase. Those of our own countrymen who hold this opinion are fond of exposing the iniquities of the old Victorian home-domination, with its tyranny and resulting repression; the famous—or infamous—Mr. Barrett of Wimpole Street is their 'patron devil'. On the other hand there are those of a more conservative cast of mind who view the modern tendency with much misgiving. They deplore the loosening of the family bond and are quick to trace the evils of juvenile delinquency to the general weakening of parental control. The great mass of the parents of our country—those who are neither left-wing liquidators nor the disciples of Mr. Barrett—waver uneasily between the two opinions. They are uncomfortably conscious that modern psychology has produced some hard knocks for unwise parents and they are haunted by the ghosts of such words as 'repressions', 'complexes', 'frustrations', and fixations'. They are aware that advanced opinion is against the family, and they feel that there must be something in it. On the other hand many of them look back to their own childhood family experiences with gratitude and affection, realising more and more as the years go by how much they owe to the matrix in which they were moulded. They halt, therefore, perpetually between two opinions, and this uncertainty makes for feebleness and vacillation. They don't quite know what to do about it, so they end up at the ultimate solution of all English folk, that of 'muddling through'.

The purpose of this little book is to consider the problem of religion in its relation to the family. This problem obviously cannot be tackled—much less solved—unless we first come to some clear conclusion about the place which the family ought to take in the general upbringing of the children under the conditions of modern society. In other words, we must make up our minds about the questions I have raised in the foregoing paragraphs before we can deal with the specific problem of religious training in the home. In the first section, therefore, I shall deal with the place of the 'family gang' in the general social scheme, deferring to the second the problems of religious education.

Part One

CHAPTER 1

BRAINS: OLD AND NEW

Our enquiry as to the true place of the family gang in the social scheme will involve us in a number of short excursions into physiology, psychology, and history, and will lead us, in the end, into the Juvenile Courts. Let us begin with the physiology.

Modern research into the nature of the human brain has revealed it as resembling in some ways one of our typical old country mansions; it is a patch-work of many periods. Just as the mansion may have a Georgian front, a Victorian conservatory, seventeenth-century kitchens, and a mediaeval dungeon beneath, so our brains contain older and newer elements, the latter representing the additions to our equipment which Nature has provided during the long process of evolution. Nature has, rather remarkably, done her job along very much the same lines as the builders of the mansion, that is to say she has proceeded by addition rather than by demolition; when she has wanted to increase the capacity and scope of the brain she has done it by adding new material rather than by expanding and altering the old. The kitchens are still used as kitchens and the store-rooms as store-rooms—and, one may add, the antique dungeons still contain some grisly relics, often quite unknown to the polite inhabitants of the spacious modern drawing-rooms. Moreover, to carry the analogy still further, Nature has installed throughout the mansion a very complete and efficient telephone system linking all the rooms, old and new, together, and it is a system on which the wrong number is never given and the line is never engaged.

The 'old brain' in man bears a strong resemblance to the brains of the higher animals, such as the dog. It contains the centres which receive and correlate the messages received through the nervous system from without—sight, hearing, touch, taste, and smell. It also contains somewhere the centres from which proceed the instincts and emotions—anger, curiosity, love, desire, pleasure and fear. This is what we should expect, since we know that these instincts and emotions also exist in the dog. The old brain is itself a composite creation, containing newer and older elements, and it is so arranged throughout that the *newer* always controls the *older*—never vice versa.

The 'new brain' is confined to man and certain of the apes, and is of course much more fully developed in the former than in the latter. It has been super-imposed upon the older brain, enclosing it and much exceeding it in bulk, and the inter-communication system between the two has been most efficiently designed. It is the seat of all conscious intellectual processes and in particular of that mysterious element, unique to man, which we call self-consciousness; and true to her guiding principle Nature has subordinated the old brain to the new—the intellect has been put in control of the instincts and emotions.

We cannot say when, or by what process, these additions to our brain equipment were made, or whether they came about by slow and almost imperceptible degrees or by some process more analogous to the additions to the country mansion; but we shall, I think, be making a fairly safe guess if we suggest that the growth of the new brain went hand-in-hand with man's growing mastery over his environment and that this mastery, in turn, was paralleled by his social organisation. Which of these was cause and which effect we cannot say, but we can assert with some confidence that our intellectual development has been due in no small degree to our social life. The 'gang' has had a good deal to do with the forging of our wits.

This physiological structure of the brain is in line with our own consciousness about the make-up of our own particular minds. We are aware that the thinking, talking, arguing, planning part of us is, as it were, 'on the surface', and that our instinctive and emotional life dwells on deeper levels. From these depths our instincts and emotions come bursting up into the daylight of our conscious minds, providing all the driving-power required for action and demanding insistently the directing control of our intellect. At times, of course, the demand of our emotions is so overwhelming that the intellect abdicates its control, as when we 'see red' or yield to some irresistible impulse. But always in these cases, when we have come to ourselves again, we recognise that our behaviour has been less than human; we have betrayed, in our abandonment of restraint, something which is an essential part of our nature as human beings—the old brain has taken charge of the new, and that is contrary to the provision of Nature.

Apart from these moments of abandonment we must also be aware, if we are honest with ourselves, that in very many cases when our instincts and emotions send up a demand to our conscious minds the control exercised by the latter is somewhat of a sham. This leads to the phenomenon which the psychologists call 'rationalisation,' when the conscious mind has to find some plausible reason for giving the emotions and instincts their head, even though the real reason is not sufficiently respectable to be admitted to the level of consciousness. The tail is really wagging the dog, but the dog, to satisfy his own self-consciousness and the demand of Nature that the new brain should control the old, has to kid himself that he is wagging the tail. Rationalisation of this kind plays a big part in the lives of most of us and is responsible for much of the folly, cruelty, and evil of mankind. We are jealous of a particular person because we feel inferior to him; we know that he is better at his job or in some respect of character than we are, so we hate him. But jealousy and hate of this kind are not respectable instincts—they do not pass the test of the moral censor which has his seat in our new brain—so our minds have to devise some other and more respectable reason for our instinctive dislike; we tell ourselves that we hate him because of his political opinions or religious views or because he wears a bow tie or went to the wrong school, or for any other of a dozen silly reasons. But honour—the honour of the new brain—is satisfied, and henceforth we can hate in peace.

It is when we come to consider the children that the importance of this distinction between the old brain and the new, between instinct and reason, becomes apparent. Children do not have to acquire those faculties which are associated with the old brain, they are endowed with them at birth, even if some of them do not show their presence till later; they do not have to *learn* to desire or fear or love, to cry for food and feel comfortable when they are filled, to turn instinctively away from strangers or to nestle happily into mother's arms. These things are born in them and the equipment, though some of it may be latent, is complete. But they *do* have to learn the faculties associated with the new brain; they can only learn them through a long and sometimes painful apprenticeship, and all the materials out of which the new brain has to create its intellectual and co-ordinating functions have to reach it through the medium of the old brain, that is through sense impressions, instincts, and emotions. During childhood the old brain is the tutor of the new, the tail is continually wagging the dog, until, bit by bit, the dog learns by experience to wag the tail.

The whole complicated process of education may be summed up as the process of teaching the new brain to attain the maximum possible degree of control over the old brain *without doing violence to it*. For we have to face the fact that this strange duality between the old and the new does introduce an element of conflict into our essential nature, just as the juxtaposition of the Georgian façade and the Elizabethan kitchen introduces an element of conflict and restlessness into the aspect of the country mansion. This conflict between the old brain and the new, between instinct and reason, is both the bane and the glory of humanity; it is responsible for man's noblest achievements and for his basest follies. And in this progressive development of the control of the new brain over the old, which I have defined as the essence of education, it *is* possible for the old to be damaged in such a way that a truly healthy and harmonious personality can never be achieved. The vital condition for health and true growth is that the communications between the old and the new should be kept alive, free, and uninterrupted. It is fatally easy for these communications to become weakened or even cut completely, and when that happens mental illness and social mal-adjustment are certain to follow. The normal provision of Nature is that instinct and emotion should have a free outlet into the upper region of the conscious mind, there to be dealt with by the fully integrated intellect, but sometimes the new brain, either from some outside suggestion or internal conflict, does not like the raw material it receives from below and solves the problem in the wrong way by cutting the communication wires and refusing to receive the messages. The instincts and emotions, thus denied their natural outlet, run amok in the deeper levels below the conscious mind and, besides causing suffering, weakness, and added conflict, often emerge in a disguised form as uncontrollable urges with which the intellectual faculties are powerless to cope. One more fact remains to be noted about children. Although elementary intellectual faculties make their appearance quite early on, and they soon learn to talk, think, and even argue, this appearance of mental activity is in some ways illusory—it does not mean that the new brain is in control in the sense in which the phrase is applicable to adults. Although it is pursuing a vigorous life of its own, full of creative fancy and experiment, the new brain is still under the tutelage of the old. *Children run almost one hundred per cent on their instincts and emotions.*

I am well aware that the foregoing is a somewhat bizarre and unscientific hotch-potch of physiology and psychology. The exact relationship between brain and mind is still one of the unsolved secrets of science; that there are molecular changes in the brain associated with thought is probable, but which is the cause and which the effect—which the tail and which the dog—is still a mystery. But there is certainly *parallelism* between the constitution of the brain and the make-up of the mind, and that is all that I wish to emphasise at the moment. At any rate I believe that the conclusions I would draw from these considerations would meet with general assent from those who are experts in the sciences involved; they are as follows :—

1. Man's instincts and emotions date from a very early period in his history, and were laid down, in their present form, before his fully-developed intellectual equipment was achieved.

2. These emotions and instincts have not been materially changed in character since the superaddition of the intellectual faculties. The conscious mind can *control* instinct and emotion, but it can neither create nor essentially modify them.

3. In young children the instincts and emotions are paramount. They take the lead in educating the developing intellect, and at any rate up to the age of puberty they are the main factor in the child's life.

CHAPTER 2

THE PRIMITIVE FAMILY GANG

If the foregoing principles are admitted we are faced immediately with the necessity for our excursion back into history, for it is clear that if instinct and emotion play so important a part in the lives of the children we shall not understand them or their needs unless we get some idea of the conditions of life under which those instincts and emotions were forged. When you come across an unfamiliar and complicated machine the first question you ask, as you examine it, is " What was it made for ? " and you will never understand an ancient building, such as a cathedral, unless you can discover what purposes were in the minds of the men who built it. The same principles applies exactly to the instinctive and emotional life of children—or of us adults for the matter of that. What was this equipment given us for ?

The experts tell us that man, as a recognisable human being, not an animal, has existed on this planet for something between half-a-million and a million years. This huge period of time may be divided roughly into three sections of very unequal length, corresponding to three stages in his social—that is his ' gang '—development. The third and latest of these stages—it is convenient for the moment to work backwards—is the stage we call civilisation, and we shall not be far wrong if we put it at something like seven or eight thousand years. It is, as its name implies, the period when man has lived in cities, or, more generally, in big communities such as towns and nations. It is the era of the large and highly complicated gang. We must remember, of course, that eight thousand years is, as far as our own ancestry is concerned, probably a gross over-statement; it is very unlikely that many of us in this country have a civilised streak in our ancestry going back for more than a couple of thousand years at most.

The next stage, still going backwards, we may call the agricultural and pastoral period, and it may extend for twenty or twenty-five thousand years back from the beginnings of civilisation. It represents the period when man had learned to till the soil and to domesticate animals as a source of food. These two activities did not, of course, necessarily go together and they resulted in very different ways of life. The primitive agriculturalists had to live in permanent settlements, while the herdsmen would be usually nomadic, wandering with their flocks over the prairies, tundras, and feeding-grounds in search of fresh pasturage. But we may bracket these activities together because in both cases man was relieved of the necessity of depending mainly on hunting for his sustenance. This is the age of what we may call, again very roughly, the village community. The primitive farmers tended to get together in small settlements for mutual support, and the nomadic herdsmen also frequently combined in groups of a similar size. As regards numbers and the complexity of group organisation we may call this the age of the ' village gang.'

Beyond and behind this second agricultural and pastoral period there stretches the immense vista of the first, or hunting age, when man depended entirely for his food-supply on the pursuit of game. During the latter part of this period, when he had acquired considerable skill in devising effective long-range weapons such as the bow, he may have combined together in groups or tribes of some sort, in certain areas, but all through the earlier stages—and in many cases right to the end—he was unquestionably a *solitary* hunter. The reason for this is quite simple ; before he had discovered long-range weapons or learned to fix a sharp nodule of flint or pointed stone to a wooden shaft to form an effective spear, man was compelled to get close to his quarry before he could kill or maim it, and large groups of people drive away the game. So, for many hundreds of thousands of years after their first appearance on this Earth, we must imagine our ancestors moving through the forests and prairies and swamps that covered the land surface of the globe in tiny, isolated groups, instinctively avoiding other groups in order that they might have an unrestricted field for their hunting. By far the greater part of this first primitive period is the age of the family gang.

The above is, of course, a very rough and inaccurate picture of the development of the human race, but for our purposes it is, I think, a valid one. For one thing we must remember that these periods were not sharply divided from one another, but existed—indeed still exist—simultaneously. The hunters lived on in many parts of the world all through the 'agricultural' age and both survived on through the period we call 'civilisation.'

What about man's brain throughout this long history? The growth of the 'new brain' with its intellectual faculties cannot at present be dated, but we can say with certainty that by the end of the first, or hunting, period man was fully endowed with his intellectual faculties and that all his larger social groupings are the product of 'new brain' activity. What is more important from the point of view of our present enquiry is the fact, of which there can be little doubt, that the old brain—with its content of instinct and emotion—is wholly the product of the earlier part of the primitive age: our—and our children's—instincts and emotions come from the time when man was a solitary hunter, they were forged and laid down in their present form, complete to the last bolt and nut, when the only gang in existence was the family gang. All the immense developments of civilisation have been impotent to modify the essential nature of these instincts and emotions of a primitive age, though the activity of the new brain has been able to direct them into new channels. The 'herd instinct' that impels ninety thousand football fans to crowd the Wembley Stadium for a Cup Final is only the extension and adaptation of the instinct that drew the little forest group to huddle together at night in the shelter of their cave, or brought them crowding with excited cries of delight round the carcase of the newly-slain buck, and the contrary instinct that impels twelve Englishmen, if they have to enter an empty train, to install themselves in twelve separate compartments is only the extension of the primitive urge of the solitary hunter to sheer away from his neighbour so as to get the forest to himself.

It may be that the apparently well-nigh insoluble problems

of modern large-scale communities, problems that lead up to the supreme folly of war, spring ultimately from this inner conflict between the old brain and the new. By instinct and emotion man is a small-gang animal, and his new brain—his intellectual powers—have led him on into regions of social organisation where his old brain cannot follow. In communities, just as in individuals, it is possible for the conscious mind to lose its connections with the unconscious, and for instinct and emotion to be either repressed and driven underground or to be exploited in ways for which they are not fitted. Communities, as well as individuals, can suffer from neurosis.

If we then accept the contention that young children whose thinking powers are not yet developed are the 'natural' products of a very early and primitive form of society we must make some effort to take, if we can, a closer look at the gang in which their instincts were formed. We can only get a very hazy, generalised view of this primitive society, but our imaginations can fill in a good many of the details from our knowledge of similar 'primitives' of our own day. We can imagine the little group moving precariously through the virgin forests, hunting and being hunted, for besides the smaller game which was their particular quarry the land was swarming with fierce and terrible beasts who were their dreaded enemies. The group might, perhaps, consist of a dozen or more persons—father, a wife or two, a handful of children, and possibly one or two attached adults such as uncles. They would make their temporary lodgments in caves, hollows scooped in the river banks, or nests rudely woven in the tops of the trees. Life would be one bitter struggle against starvation, food being almost the sole topic of thought and conversation. We have gone back, as I have already suggested, far beyond the invention of the bow and spear, and the only weapons would be stones, clubs, and throwing-sticks. It is unlikely that fire had yet been discovered—or rather adapted to human use, since the volcano must have often been a familiar sight. Almost anything would be welcomed as food, including insects, grubs, and roots, and we of to-day would be as revolted by our ancestors' feeding methods as we should by most of their other personal habits.

Let us take a look at the children. Up to the age of seven or eight—that is till they had acquired some mastery over their limbs—they would be left in the charge of the women, as the young have been since the foundation of the world. But as soon as they could run and use their hands they would be wanted—needed as active members of the gang, for there would be no room for passengers in that storm-tossed crew. The boys, probably, would be taken in hand by the men, and the girls by the women, to be taught their various jobs. Food being the main preoccupation of the gang the boys would be taught, one may presume, to hunt and to kill while the girls attended to the roots and fruit, besides lending a hand with the younger children. The girls found their dolls ready-made in those days.

We can follow in imagination the education of the boys. Under the charge of father or a grown-up brother—or possibly Uncle Harry—they would be taught to read a trail, to glide through the undergrowth like a shadow, to climb rocks and trees like a cat, and—above all—to throw stones. All day long they would throw—throw—throw, and there was nothing in the whole wide world, the persons of their immediate kin excepted, at which it was not lawful for them to throw a stone. And they would be taught to kill, as the chief aim of their life. Every living thing was an object for their stones and sticks, for every living thing—with a very few exceptions—was potential food. They would learn, too, to share what they killed; every animal they were lucky enough to knock over must be brought back—with what pride !—to the family store. They would learn to watch, and to keep quiet, lying by the hour on their faces without moving a muscle, enduring the stings of poisonous insects. Perhaps most important of all, they would learn to fear, for fear was one of the most valuable defensive weapons in the primitive hunter's armoury. They would learn to fear the dark, when they could not see the approach of an enemy beast, and to fear the slightest sign of pursuit. Since their life would depend, in a double sense, upon their speed they would learn to run faster and faster—every day they would be exercising their bodies feverishly in the attempt to knock another second off the hundred yards and add another yard to their throw. And at every point their cunning and wits—that exercise of the new brain which was developing in them—would be perfectly linked with instinct and emotion. The gang, or communal, sense would be stronger than we, with our highly individualised minds, can imagine today. Self-consciousness was developing, but it was growing out of gang consciousness, not vice versa. The instinct of gang-solidarity, of gang-obedience, would be deeply rooted in them, and there would be no need to teach them to follow a lead—that would be innate in them. But the leadership—the mastery—which they wanted would be of a special kind, it would be leadership in a very small group. Perhaps two of them would be taught together, perhaps three, but hardly more. You cannot teach bird-watching today in classes of fifty—the birds all fly away.

So they would grow up to the age of puberty, at full stretch physically during the whole period, learning a man's job and, from the beginning, active and useful members of the small gang. Whether they ' played ' or not, in the sense that modern children play, we do not know, but from our own observation of puppies we may guess that they did, and that their play would be an extension of their work. If they played at hide-and-seek it would be because hiding and seeking were part of their job as hunters, and if they indulged in leap-frog it would be because leaping was one of their ' school subjects '.

And during all this time, right through their education, there would be no other social group than their own family within their ken. They might be dimly aware that miles away across the hills another little group like theirs was engaged on similar tasks, but they would have no interest in this group except that it was to be avoided. There would be little, if any, fighting in that primitive life. Sometimes two hunters from different groups might meet over the body of a buck and settle its ownership in the time-honoured fashion, but that would be all. The next hunting-group would be a gang to be avoided, not attacked. Perhaps, when he was of an age for it, the youth would scout furtively round the outskirts of a neighbouring gang, drawn by some inexplicable instinct, till he saw a girl that suited his fancy. Then for many days he would stalk her till the opportunity came of 'cutting her out' from her companions and persuading her, by cajolery or by force, to come away with him and be his mate, then, perhaps, after a farewell feast, a new little gang might after a while make its way off into the forest, leaving the old companions and the old surroundings for ever.

This is a fanciful reconstruction and I do not suggest that we should take it too seriously or attach much importance to its details, but something of the kind must have been the normal way of life of our primitive ancestors, and that for a period to be measured not by thousands but by hundreds of thousands of years. It is the length of this formative period which it is so important to grasp. You may, if you care to, substitute a visual picture in order to grasp the significance of this immense duration, since mere numbers are always dead and unimaginative things. As you read these pages you are, more than probably, sitting in an ordinary room, some eight feet high. Just cast your eye at the wall for a moment, at some spot where it is unencumbered by furniture, and let your glance run up it from floor to ceiling. Imagine that the whole height represents the long career of man on this planet, from his first recognisable appearance by the floor to the present day at the ceiling. Then the third period I have mentioned—the period of civilisation—would be represented by the width of a penny stamp, stuck sideways on the wall with its top edge touching the ceiling. Imagine next a post-card stuck below the stamp, also laid sideways and touching the stamp with its upper edge; that represents the second period, the agricultural and pastoral age. And the whole height of the wall below stands for the hunting period—the age of the family gang! And remember that we have taken a conservative estimate of the antiquity of man, actually we might have to imagine the wall continued down for several yards below the floor to get the true scale. And all through that long stretch of time, just as the seas were slowly depositing on their beds the silt from ten thousand streams till it hardened under pressure into the sedimentary rocks that tower on the mountains today, so the innermost emotions of man were being laid down out of the infinite, and infinitely repeated, experiences of his myriad days, until they hardened by the pressure of habit into the unchangeable thing we call human nature.

Before we leave this primitive and pregnant family group there are two points we should note about it for future comparisons. In the first place it was probably a *larger* group than the great majority of modern families. Quite apart from the possibility of polygamy, infant and child mortality must have been very high, and the 'expectation of life' of the adults very short. Not very many people in those days would live much beyond the age of forty—at any rate not many men—, and any man to-day who has played Rugby football will know the reason why. Before you are forty you begin to lose both speed and staying-power, and to lose these, under such conditions, was to lose your life. We may imagine, then, that the children of that age would probably grow up in a family of at least a dozen souls.

The second point to notice—and it is one of great importance —is that the gap between children and parents, in both physical and mental age, was much narrower than to-day. In those far-off times when the new brain was in its infancy the mental superiority of the parents over the children would be small. And the sense of community in the group would be much stronger, not only because all the members were engaged on the same job—father in those days did not disappear on the 8.55 to some mysterious business in the City—but because the sense of self-consciousness and of individuality lies in the new brain, not the old, and the further we go back into pre-history the weaker we shall find the sense of individuality and the stronger the sense of community. Man was a social animal before he was an individual, and we must never forget that tiny children have to fight for their individuality, as their self-consciousness wakens to life, not only against outside domination but against some of the deepest instincts of their own natures. This is the cause of many childish difficulties; Mr. Barrett of Wimpole Street is not the only nigger in the family woodpile.

But it is time for us to quit the primeval forest and pay our promised visit to the Juvenile Court.

CHAPTER 3
YOUNG GANGSTERS

A great deal of valuable information about ordinary things is often obtained by studying extraordinary things. The apparently mad behaviour of one insignificant little planet led Einstein to the formulation of his famous theory of Relativity, which has revolutionised Science; the study of acute disease in hospitals has led to much knowledge about the minor ailments of normal healthy people, and it was from the behaviour of insane people in asylums that modern psychology has learned the principles that govern your mind and mine. The same is true about children; we can find out many useful facts about the jolly, normal, every-day children who throng our schools and streets by giving a little thought to the behaviour of the abnormal youngsters of whom we read in the reports of the Juvenile Courts. We shall also—and this is important for our present purpose—obtain some valuable side-lights on the 'family gang' in modern life.

Juvenile delinquency—to use that horrible phrase which adults have coined, with their usual complacency, to fob off on to other people the sins for which they are largely responsible themselves—is no new thing, but the recent wise reform by which children's cases are segregated and dealt with in special courts has brought it more into the limelight. This is not wholly good, but at any rate it has enabled interested people to study its problems with greater ease and certainty.

There are, in the main, three types of young criminal, only one of which is important for our present purpose. The first type is the genuine crook, the boy or girl who is born with a 'kink', the child who starts life with a diseased mind just as others are born with diseased bodies. There are a certain number of these and they occur in all ranks of society; they are essentially a job for specialists, needing special treatment, special homes, and special schools, and I do not propose to say more about them here. The second type is the boy or girl who appears quite normal, comes from an average good home and is doing reasonably well at school, but for one reason or another yields to a sudden temptation and commits a crime which brings him or her into court. An actual instance will help us to understand this type better than pages of general description. Two or three years ago a boy of eleven was brought up before the Juvenile Court in a provincial town on a charge of stealing two pound-notes from a girl's hand-bag, lying unattended on the counter of a shop. At first the case seemed puzzling, since the boy came from a respectable and wisely-conducted home and bore an excellent character at school, but when it was investigated the following facts were discovered. Some eighteen months before the offence was committed this particular boy had become infected with the 'fishing' germ—a disease which has been known to attack even Prime Ministers and Bishops—and since then had spent every moment he could spare over his hobby. Now it so happened that in a certain shop-window in the town there was hanging a beautiful shiny fishing-rod, replete—as the house-agents say—with all the most desirable fittings and gadgets, and priced at fifty shillings. Every morning and evening for weeks, on his way to and from school, that boy had flattened his nose against the shop-window, gazing hungrily at the object of all his desires. He had somehow managed to scrape together the odd ten shillings, but the two pounds was beyond him, and he could see no prospect of getting it till suddenly, out of the blue, he was faced with that overwhelming temptation and fell to it. The Magistrates, I am glad to say, realised that they were not dealing with a criminal and put him on probation; he had received a thorough shaking-up and, so far as I know, has gone straight ever since.

Now that boy, not to put too fine a point on it, is you and me. He is the ordinary citizen who does now and then, in spite of the best intentions, make a fool of himself and run off the rails. Most of us probably, if we take a candid peep back into our own childhood, can remember—I hope not without a blush—one or more occasions when we did something correspondingly lawless which, if there had happened to be a policeman behind the hedge or peeping round the door, might have landed us into Court. We are all sons of Adam and inherit Grandfather's weakness for stolen fruit in some form. The best of family trainings, the wisest and most liberal of schoolings, are not fool-proof and the best of mortals is liable at times to be a fool. Happy are we if, on such occasions, we fell into the hands of those in whom the quality of mercy is not strained.

The last, and from our point of view most important, type of young offender is the 'gangster,' and he is by far the greatest problem to the authorities, causing them more and worse headaches than both the other types put together. If you talk to the Probation Officer or the Police Inspector about them they will tell you, as likely as not, that they are at their wits' end to know what to do with them. They are as hard as glass, nothing seems to scratch them, to get under their skin; they are susceptible to no appeal; devoid, apparently, of public or private conscience. And they go wrong again and again—not just once, like the lad with (or rather, alas, *without*) the fishing rod. So far from yielding to a sudden temptation they seem to go round looking for it—with extraordinary success. The peak age for this juvenile gangsterism is apparently thirteen years, and by far the greater number are boys; girls for some mysterious and probably very important reason, are not affected in the same way. And the gangs in which they work are nearly always small—two or three, or four, seldom larger. As for their crimes, they include of course all the usual mischief of fruit-stealing and petty theft to which all small boys are more or less liable, together with other offences which are more sinister.

The young gangsters' crimes are nearly always marked by a complete lack of social sense, and it is that which makes it so difficult to bring any moral appeal home to them. They will, of course, strip the fruit from the rich man's orchard, but they will also rob the two or three gooseberry-bushes belonging to the poor old cottager who has the greatest difficulty in making ends meet; they will smash the windows and fences of the desirable family

residence, but they will also—and apparently with equal pleasure—
destroy the seats and swings in the public children's park. Two
such gangs were laid by the heels not long ago in different parts
of the country; one had on several occasions placed heavy stones
and iron bars across the railway line and the other had rigged up
an ingenious device with cords and pulleys for dragging at the
signal-wires on the railway in such a way that a signal set at danger
could be pulled off, allowing the train to pass. The aim of both
gangs was the same, they wanted to stage a train-wreck so that they
could enjoy the thrill of it. There have also been many cases of
cruelty to domestic animals—a vice that one does not usually
associate with normal boys. Hens and ducks have been stoned
and either maimed or killed, sheep have been injured, and even
cattle attacked—and in one case blinded. And this juvenile
gangsterism, remember, is going on all over the country to a
greater or lesser extent: if you come across one place which
appears to be free of it you will probably hear a bitter complaint
if you talk to the police-sergeant in the next village. For this is a
village problem as well as an urban; there may be more gangsterism in the great cities simply because there are more children
and the facilities for healthy play are fewer, but the country
districts do not escape their share. I do not want to exaggerate
the problem of juvenile gangsterism, but with all respect to those
who say that it is much over-publicised I still maintain that it is
a serious matter and the sign of a serious malaise in our modern
civilisation. It is sometimes said that gangsterism is a phase
through which many youngsters pass and they grow out of it in
time to become worthy citizens; it would be pleasant if we could
believe this to be true, but the litter on our commons and beauty-
spots after a holiday, the filthy scrawling in railway-carriages and
public lavatories, the wholesale pilfering on the railways and
elsewhere, the readiness to cheat in public and private dealings,
tell a different story. The young gangsters, as they grow up, may
learn out of self-defence to conform outwardly to the more obvious
standards of society, but the reform is no more than skin deep.
Ask any hotel-keeper in a big town his opinion about the honesty

of his clients and how far he is prepared to trust them with the towels, soap, and tea-spoons.

Some years ago I became connected, for a while, with a village where this 'young gangster' trouble existed in an acute form. Most of the fathers and mothers were busily at work all day in small local factories, reaching home at seven o'clock in the evening after a tedious bus ride. The children came out of school at four, and for three hours were left to their own devices. There were no Scouts, Guides, or Clubs, and the Churches confined themselves exclusively to 'soul-saving' activities—they had no time to spare, apparently, for such trifles as minds and bodies. When I consulted the village Police Sergeant about the young gangsters he took off his helmet, mopped his brow, and expressed himself with some heat. "They wants a dam' good hiding, Sir!" was the burden of his remarks, "But there's nobody to give it 'em!" That, I discovered, was also the opinion of the majority of the villagers, particularly the gardeners and fruit-growers. By no means all of the boys, of course, were of the gangster type, many came from good homes and were naturally law-abiding, but there was a hard core of young scoundrels who set the pace for the rest, did most of the mischief, and gave the whole body of youth in the village a bad name.

I had read many of the books written about juvenile delinquency —all written, apparently, by law-abiding adults of blameless character—so there seemed only one thing to be done if I were really to understand the problem from the inside; I must become a young gangster myself. This, aided by good fortune and certain vivid memories of my own youthful misdeeds which I still, I am afraid, recall with enjoyment, I was presently able to achieve, and I found myself before long admitted to the companionship of as merry a set of young outlaws as ever infested Sherwood. One or two of them had already made acquaintance with the Juvenile Court, and their comments on, and attitude to, that august body were illuminating and shattering.

Since my primary object was to find out rather than to reform I decided that the first essential was not to be shocked, and that though it might sometimes be necessary to exercise a veto, I would refrain from lecturing. Only a few, as I have already said, were of the real ' gangster ' type, and my observations must be understood as applying only to them, not to the more law-abiding members of the gang.

The first thing that shocked me about them was their apparent cruelty. As we wandered up to the hills and woods where we played our ' Commando' games—Red Indians are hopelessly out of date—they kept a sharp eye open for living things, and every living thing was quite automatically something to be destroyed. A young fledgling, fallen out of the nest, had to be smashed with a stick. If you saw a butterfly on a flower in the hedge you dashed at it with your cap, knocked it down on the road, and squashed it with your boot. Every bird was a mark for a stone, and even the dragon-flies were something to kill. All this was done, as it were, in a friendly spirit and without animosity—it was just the normal thing to do. When I asked if they didn't have ' nature ' lessons in school the answer was a scornful " Pooh ! That's all soft ! " This seemed to be their general attitude to school teaching of all kinds, it was something to be ignored or dismissed with scorn. I knew that some of their teachers were able and intelligent people, so clearly something had gone badly wrong ; these boys were not responding in the least to their school influence, it was not touching their instinctive and emotional life.

Some of the ' toughs ' discussed their fruit-stealing escapades quite openly, going into much interesting detail of technique. They knew all the holes in the fences, suitable lines of retreat, and the personal habits of the owners. The gooseberry bushes of one old dame who lived in an isolated cottage on the hill were particularly sought after, but when I ventured to suggest that she was poor and could not afford to lose her fruit I met with no response. " That don't matter ! " was the only comment.

Another interesting fact was the bitter sense of hostility against neighbouring villages, and their boy inhabitants in particular. Under no circumstances would they admit a stranger to the Club— we had become a Club by that time—and if one from an outlying district did happen to join he was soon driven away again. They had no desire, either, to explore the territory of neighbouring communities; "That quarry belongs to Hogs-Norton," they would say, "We don't want to play there!"

All this was very distressing, but there was another side to the picture. However anti-social these young gangsters might be in respect of the community at large, and of neighbouring groups, within the circle of their own gang they were loyal, law-abiding (to the gang law), sporting, generous, and trustworthy. I have left my coat, with money and tempting valuables such as a pocket-knife in the pockets, under a tree for a whole afternoon with boys playing about and myself far away hiding, under the guise of a German parachutist, in a ditch, and nothing has ever been taken. I have left food—bags of buns, and on one occasion, when such things were still obtainable, an iced chocolate cake with a ravishing ball of pink icing on the top—with the same result. When I returned the ball of icing was still in its place, triumphant witness to the power of gang morality. On another occasion we were crossing a muddy stream over the precarious bridge formed by a fallen tree when a small urchin of eight, a newly-joined member, let out a piercing wail—"I've dropped me shillin' in the water!" So he had, and it had disappeared for ever in the mud. But before I could get across to comfort him three or four of these same gangsters had run up to him with outstretched hands full of coppers, and the loss had been made good. There was a positive as well as a negative side to the gang morality.

The tentative extension of this personal gang morality to the outside world came about in an interesting way. After a time the boys—as always happens—got tired of nothing but games and wanted to do a job of some kind. They suggested that they should form a 'Junior Service Squad'—these were a good deal in the air at that time—and offer their services to work in the gardens of people who needed help. But here I put my foot down firmly. "No!" I said, "You can't do that. What about 'nicking'? You can't go and work in people's gardens as a Club Service Squad and then 'nick' their fruit!" There was some expostulation at this, but they saw the point and retired to discuss it among themselves. Presently the ring-leader returned to report. "We've decided that there ain't going to be no ' nicking ' on Tuesdays and Saturdays ! " he announced. This was an ' interim ethic ' with a vengeance, but I accepted it, and so far as I know it was loyally observed. They did not steal from the gardens where they worked, and they did not steal on the Service Squad days ; the gang morality was beginning, in a small way, to be extended to a wider society.

It is no part of my present purpose to write a treatise on juvenile delinquency, still less on the running of Boys' Clubs, and I only record these experiences because of the light they throw on our main problem. These lads formed their own gang *because society had failed to give them the gang for which they were, emotionally and instinctively, designed.* And in doing so they had been true to their nature, both their activities and their morality were based on the primitive age from which they ' dated ' ; they had gone back to the prehistoric hunting period which we considered in the last chapter.

It is astonishing how much of the behaviour of these young twentieth-century gangsters reflected, quite unconsciously on their part, the life of a quarter of a million years ago. Their instinct to destroy or capture every living thing, their passion for throwing stones, their suspicion of the next village group, their instinct to keep themselves isolated, their complete lack of any sense of private property, and above all their insensitiveness to the existence of any other social group but their own gang—all these were a distinct inheritance from the age of the solitary hunter when the family gang was the only gang in existence. The trouble is that these young hunters of today are born into a society which, though it wants them, does not need them. When the strong gang instinct develops in them and they begin to want to ' be about father's business ' their families are apt to fail them, and they are thrown too young into a society which is far too big for them and has little use for them. Just when they are ready to be roped into the firm, to become active and essential members of a small, living community, modern society puts them into the chilly cold-storage of the Elementary school, where they are set to learn lessons that have nothing to do with hunting, and little enough, on the surface, with real life, in classes of fifty or more. Now this, in all seriousness, is just preposterous nonsense; you can give the 'new brain' a certain amount of mass-instruction in a class of fifty, very inefficiently, but you cannot educate, you cannot touch the instincts and emotions, you cannot teach or inculcate 'social sense' under such conditions. These children are designed to learn their social relationships in a very small group; that is the only gang to which, emotionally, they can respond, and others beside myself must have been dismayed at a Government pronouncement recently issued expressing the intention to reduce elementary—or primary—classes to forty and secondary school classes to thirty. This is just sheer stupidity; it is the young children who most need the smaller classes, not the adolescents. So long as we are content to give the young children this cheap and shoddy substitute for real education, so long we shall have young gangsters to worry us—and it will serve us right. Juvenile delinquency is very largely the result of the senile stupidity of us grown-ups, and when the young hunters form, in self-defence, their own 'natural' gangs in accordance with their instincts, all we can say about them is that they need " a dam' good hiding ! "

We have now, I think, accumulated the material which we set out to collect and are in a better position to consider the place of the family in modern social life. I shall attempt this task in the next chapter.

CHAPTER 4

THE NEW FAMILY GANG

The family is under a cloud in these modern days, as I pointed out in the introduction; the extreme left-wing reformers say that it is a pernicious institution, leading to the economic and emotional exploitation of the children, and the right-wingers deplore its almost complete disappearance as an influence for good in the national life. These two opinions may be mutually contradictory, but at any rate they both imply a vote of censure on the family as it is at present. If we accept the contention in the last chapter that the failure of the family is one of the main causes of so-called juvenile delinquency we are adding our own vote to the general disapproval.

Why is the modern family failing in this way? We can find the answer to the question—or at any rate some of the many answers—if we compare the modern family set-up to the primitive family gang. The modern family differs from the primitive in certain very fundamental respects, some of which we have touched on already. In the first place the primitive family gang was an occupational and economic unit as well as an emotional one—indeed, the emotional side as represented by demonstrative affection and parental 'love' was probably very rudimentary. All this is now changed, and the change set in many centuries ago. The family has ceased — except in comparatively few cases—to be an occupational unit in which the children are active partners, and the effect on the parents has been almost as disastrous as on the children. Instead of being leaders the parents have become possessors, the occupational partnership has given place to an emotional dictatorship. This, of course, is what was wrong with Mr. Barrett of Wimpole Street; if he had needed the co-operation of his family in tilling a market-garden or even hawking boot-laces round Grosvenor Square he would never have become the tyrant who kept his gifted daughter practically locked in a darkened room till, at the age of forty, she was driven to the desperate expedient of marrying a poet.

We must face the fact squarely that modern industrial civilisation has knocked on the head the family as an occupational unit except in a very few cases, such as farmers and market gardeners, and that all the King's horses and all the King's men will not put that particular Humpty-Dumpty together again. We cannot all become hunters in the illimitable forest again, even if we wanted to. Most of the family occupations which made the partnership of the primitive family possible are now provided for us by the State in one form or another. The water, which the children used to fetch from the spring, is now available by turning on a tap in the scullery; the food which had to be hunted and skinned is brought to the door in a tin, and the same applies to the fuel (if any), the bread, and the fruit. Even the house itself is provided ready-made by the builder, whereas the primitive nest or cave was doubtless a piece of communal effort; all that the modern family has to do is to keep the house clean, and cleanliness, as those who have the care of children find out quickly enough, is *not* necessarily one of the primary instincts of the young—it is a 'new-brain' notion which has to be acquired gradually by the discipline of experience.

These profound changes in the status of the family have affected parents, children, and society as a whole. We may sum up their effect on the parents by stating that the old natural bond of leadership and partnership has been replaced by an unnatural bond of emotional possessiveness. The effect on the children has been to deprive them, between the age of seven and thirteen, of the sense of partnership and co-operation for which they are designed and which is a vital factor in their social education. The effect on Society as a whole has been more indirect, but even more disastrous; it has resulted in the sex instinct being divorced from the family instinct. When the word 'sex' is mentioned today you may take it almost for granted that it refers solely to the erotic passion of a man and a woman for each other—it has little to do with the founding and running of a family gang. Even in Victorian times, when the family was more strongly entrenched than it is today, ninety per cent. of the sentimental love-stories ended with the wedding bells, and few of the remainder got further than the christening of the first-born son. Modern books on sex suffer from the same limitation, even when they pretend to treat the subject in a serious spirit; they deal with the problem as if it were something which merely concerned a man and a woman. In primitive times—that is, in the period when we human beings were being made—the act of mating was merely the preliminary, and the concomitant, to a prolonged adventure in co-operation, the adventure of the family gang. Modern thought and modern writing on sex are about as sensible as would be a household cookery-book which dealt exclusively with the preparation of 'hors d'oeuvres'. We shall never recover a healthy attitude to sex, or be able to talk sense about it, till it is tied up once more, as it was always intended to be, with the family gang adventure.

The time has now come when we must take the bull by the horns and state roundly our conclusions about the future of the family in the modern world. It will be most convenient to attempt this, I think, in the form of a 'catechism'—that is by posing questions and giving the answers to them. I am well aware of the pitfalls attached to this method—it is easy for the author to restrict himself to those questions to which he thinks he has an answer ready—but I will try to play fair and to heckle myself with sufficient point and vigour. Up, then, on the soap-box, and let the heckler do his worst!

Heckler: Are the left-wingers right in regarding the family as an out-moded institution which ought to be liquidated as far as possible?

Author: No, they are wrong. Children's instinctive and emotional nature being what it is, a strong family bond up to the age of puberty is a vital necessity.

H. But surely children can learn social sense in other groups than the family? Cannot nursery schools, crêches, and primary schools do the job as well or better?

A. No, they cannot do it at all. The child's social emotions and instincts are indissolubly bound up with its parents, and you cannot alter them.

H. I see. So you would abolish nursery schools and all such institutions for young children?

A. Far from it! They are admirable institutions and may do much good *provided that they build on the foundation of the family.*

H. That sounds a bit contradictory to me; at what age, then, can children begin to profit by these other ' gangs '?

A. As soon as you like. By all means let them begin to experience other groups as soon as possible, only the family gang must come first and must remain the strongest influence up to the age of puberty.

H. So you believe in all this Victorian heavy stuff, and would like to go back to it?

A. Not a bit of it! The Victorian family, so called, was as vicious and un-natural as is your ultra-modern, liquidated, collectivised affair. I wouldn't go back to it for worlds. We've got to go *on*, not *back*.

H. Explain yourself. What was wrong with the Victorian family—from your point of view?

A. Practically everything. For one thing, the Victorian parental domination was all wrong, both emotionally and economically. But why, by-the-way, do you call it Victorian? That sort of thing was even more marked in the eighteenth century than in the nineteenth, and worse still in the seventeenth. Go and read up your social history!

H. It was you who first mentioned the Victorian family! Why quarrel with *me* about it?

A. You are quite right. In fact, we are both right; it is true that what we call the Victorian family had existed for many centuries, but it was not till the nineteenth century, with its enormous extension of the middle class as a result of industrialism, that this type of family organisation became a ' large scale ' affair. Till then the peasant type of family, based far more on co-operative effort, had been dominant in the country.

H. I see. So you regard the reforms of Lord Shaftesbury, by which children were saved from being exploited in the factories, as a retrograde step, since they prevented the children from earning their own living and being 'partners' in the family?

A. No. The exploitation of children in that way was a terrible evil and was rightly stopped. At the same time I am bound to admit that in certain respects, especially in 'emotional tone', the proletarian family of those days was likely to be healthier than the family of today.

H. Then all this legislation and reform of the last hundred years, by which children have been removed from industry and put to school instead, hasn't been a mistake?

A. No, of course it hasn't. But it has, largely owing to our ignorance of the fundamental instincts of children, created certain new problems in their development of 'social sense' resulting in juvenile delinquency and a wrong attitude, later on, to sex. And it's high time that society faced up to these problems and tackled them on sound lines.

H. What do you mean by 'sound lines'? You can't go back to the primitive family gang again, and start running about naked in the woods!

A. No, of course you can't. But we have got brains, and it's up to us to use our wits and devise a way of re-creating the new family gang in a form which will be in line with the children's instincts and emotions, and at the same time fit in with and reinforce modern society. And the problem is becoming more and more urgent, every extension of the school-leaving age—excellent in itself—will prolong childhood and increase the sense of frustration, postponing still further the consciousness of being active and needed partners in society.

H. How do you propose to re-create the family gang?

A. Now you've let yourself in for another lecture, so you'd better sit down and be quiet. I would tackle the job in a number of ways. The first essential is knowledge—not the knowledge of a few experts or pundits, but knowledge shared by the great mass of the people, the rank and file of the parents of the country.

This means adult education on a large and popular scale. We must all know the facts, and understand the problem and the issues at stake. We must understand the stock from which we are sprung and the conditions of life—the primitive family gang—under which our children's instincts and emotions were laid down. Then, next, there must be a revolution in housing. We *must* at all costs, have houses that will allow of decent-sized families for the great mass of the people. We should aim, as a national policy, for families of not less than four children, with six as an ideal. Then these families must be given social security, and that, of course, is a job for the experts—I don't pretend to be competent———

H. Stop a minute! Aren't you being rather hard on the parents of only children? Where do they come in?

A. I'm not sure that they come in at all—not into the 'natural' scheme of Nature. But there's no need for them to despair, they will just have to use their wits a bit more energetically than the others in order to provide the true gang life for their solitary chick, that's all.

H. All right—carry on! You were saying . . . ?

A. I was saying that good housing and social security were necessary preliminaries to the new family gang adventure, but they are only preliminaries. The really vital thing is a completely new conception, in the minds of the parents, about the meaning of love and marriage; these have got to be caught up into and made part of the family adventure, so that the one is carried over into the other. It implies nothing short of a spiritual revolution.

H. You talk a lot about 'adventure', what do you mean by it?

A. Don't you see? The old primitive type of communal adventure, the kind of thing I described in Chapter 2, is no longer possible in the modern world so each family will have to provide a substitute for it that will satisfy the emotional demands of the children—and it must be a genuine substitute, nothing sham or 'phoney' will do. It must be real, co-operative adventure and effort together in all sorts of activity and all kinds of projects, and these things must be part of the family life—necessary for its happiness and existence—if the children's urge to be needed as well as wanted is to be satisfied.

H. That's all very vague—can't you give a definite programme for us to bite on?

A. That's exactly what I *can't* do. I can't plan for the family in No. 2 Utopia Villas, Heaven-on-Thames—and no more can you. They can't use our wits, they've got to use their own, in working it all out. The one essential is that they should really regard their own family gang adventure as being by far the most important, the most interesting, and the most absorbing thing that life holds for them; if they feel like that, their own native wits will tell them how to work it out. But it's going to mean a lot of mental effort and real self-sacrifice.

H. What do you mean by self-sacrifice?

A. Well, let's take a look at a certain family I know, with three children between the ages of eight and thirteen. As a matter of fact one of them is one of the ' young gangsters ' I was talking about in the last chapter. Father isn't in the Forces, he's working long hours in a munition factory some distance from his home, and mother too, since the children all go to school, has got a job in another factory. They get home, pretty tired, between half-past-six and seven, and when they've had tea—what happens? I'll tell you what happens; on Monday night there's a whist-drive at the British Legion, and it's " Run off and play, kids, and don't get into mischief! Your mother and I are going to the whist-drive!" Tuesday it's a darts competition at the Dog and Duck, and they both go off again. Wednesday's a dance at the Club, on Thursdays they go to the pictures—taking the children with them if it's a good gangster film—Friday's another whist-drive, and on Saturday there's a dance at the Parish Hall. Now I haven't a word to say against any of these amusements, those people work hard and deserve their recreation, but I do say that those children are not having a square deal—that family is not a family gang on any count.

H. Don't you believe in play for children, then? Surely those kids are happy enough larking about by themselves?

A. Of course they want some play, and by all means let us provide many more play-grounds for city children to take the place of the forests and streams for which they were intended, but we moderns have made a ghastly mistake in thinking that the only thing children need in their spare time is 'play'. As I have said already, they want to be *needed*; they would far rather hear us say "Come and do this job with me!" than "Run away and play!"

H. You haven't yet given a hint as to what sort of jobs you mean.

A. That will depend entirely on the family, and must be left to the wits of the individual parents—I have said already that yours and mine cannot do the job for them. But I know of one family where the father is a stone-mason, working in a quarry. He has rigged up a shed in his tiny garden and teaches his boys, in the evenings, to carve all manner of funny little figures out of odd bits of stone. You can see them stuck up all over the garden (and aren't the boys proud of them!) and now they are giving them away to the neighbours. Then there's another house I have heard of where the two girls are very clever at drawing and all the rooms are hung with their pictures. Dad and brother Jim together make the frames on a portable bench they rig up over the scullery sink, and as the girls are constantly scrapping the old pictures and making better ones of a different size there's always plenty of work for the men. I know of another family where the three girls—all under 15—take it in turns to prepare and cook one complete meal each every week, each on her own. The parents never know what's coming, of course, and sometimes I expect the results are a bit startling! Then in another family I know the two boys are in the catapult stage and father, instead of frowning on it and telling them not to get into mischief, has made a catapult for himself and they all go off together for target practice (not to mention a stray rabbit ot two) in an old quarry, on Saturday afternoons. Another family—boys and girls together

—go tree-climbing with father, while mother sits under another tree with the picnic basket and shudders quietly till they all come down safely. Then some families breed rabbits as a communal effort, others run an allotment, and I heard of one which made a substantial sum of money by growing tomatoes in a home-made green-house and used it to colour-wash every room in the house (as well as their own persons) from top to bottom, every member of the family joining in both occupations. Wise parents will be constantly on the look-out for new projects, with an eye to the special aptitudes and needs of their children. Some of these projects will be 'occupational' and some sporting or recreative, but the guiding principle in all will be partnership—to make the children feel that they are needed for the success of the family adventure.

H. I guess that you are a countryman! What about the millions of city-dwellers? It will not be easy for them to find many of these opportunities for adventure, as you call it.

A. That is quite true, and here, surely, there is a big opening for a new kind of Club or Community Centre, catering specially for the complete family gang and offering facilities for families to pursue their special interests as a group. The Peckham Health Centre was an interesting pioneer venture on these lines.

H. What about all these modern Youth Clubs? Don't they cut across this family gang idea of yours?

A. To some extent they do, in the sense that if the families were all they ought to be these Clubs and similar organisations would not be needed to the same extent. As it is, they are trying to do the job which ought to be done by the family and to undo the harm which bad families have caused.

H. There would still be a place, then, for Youth Clubs in your hypothetical 'Heaven-on-Thames', where all the families are ideal family gangs?

A. Most certainly there would, though they might be organised on somewhat different lines. The family gang is a beginning—it isn't an end. Our children have to learn to belong to the bigger society, and the sooner they begin to do so the better, provided that they have a firm start in the family gang. I hope that there will be any number of Clubs, Societies, and Gangs of all sorts in Heaven-on-Thames, through which the children can move freely, learning to apply and develop the sense of citizenship they have learned in their own families. But you must start with the family, if the children do not learn the elements of citizenship there, where they are designed to learn it, they won't be likely to make good citizens of the bigger 'new brain' communities.

H. What will the schools be like in Heaven-on-Thames?

A. For the younger children they will be essentially 'gang' schools, with small classes, where the children can receive the individual attention and personal leadership which their nature demands. There will be no 'mass-instruction' of children in Heaven-on-Thames—we shall have a local bye-law, you see, that the Director of Education shall be publicly hanged in the market-square if a class of more than twenty children is discovered in any school under his control.

H. Indeed! Well, you have dealt with family and school; is there anything else to be said?

A. Yes. Somehow—I don't quite know in what way—society as a whole has got to show the children that they are needed as well as wanted. It has got to get them into the firm and give them vital jobs to do, making them feel that they are part of the working community and not mere ornaments or nuisances, as they are at present. I know of one gang of little outlaws who, under a wise leader, have turned a bit of waste ground in the middle of their village into a rest-garden, complete with home-made seats, and who have undertaken to keep it in order. I would venture to bet that none of the boys who have helped over that job will ever get into the Children's Court for damaging the trees in a a public park! Why shouldn't that—or something of the kind—be done in every town and village in the land? Why shouldn't the children be recognised by every Parish and Urban Council as being useful partners in society, with certain interesting jobs to do—under expert leadership, of course, but they are ready enough to follow a lead—the results of which they can see and be proud of ? And why shouldn't the children have a hand in all this planning that is so much in the news ? Why not get *their* ideas as to what London or Birmingham or Bristol should be like when they are rebuilt ? They are quite capable of drawing plans, and they might have one or two valuable suggestions to make— " Out of the mouth of babes . . . ", you know !

H. Good gracious ! So Heaven-on-Thames is to be town-planned by the children ! I guess there will be an inordinate number of sweet-shops and ice-cream bars !

A. Possibly. But there will be very few police courts and only one very small prison—marked, like the less desirable films, " For Adults Only."

Part Two

CHAPTER 5

PRIMITIVE RELIGION; AND PARENTS

The religious instinct in man is one of his oldest items of equipment and dates back, along with his other emotions, to the days of the primitive family gang. How or why it developed we do not know, but from the earliest dawnings of his self-consciousness man seems to have had an itch, or an instinct, to link himself with powers outside himself, whether those powers were, to his thinking, hostile or friendly.

We need not concern ourselves in these pages with the various forms under which this primitive religion expressed itself. That they took the shape, to our modern minds, of superstition and magic is not important; what is important is to understand something of the instinct that lay behind them. It would be as great a folly to deny the reality of primitive man's religious instinct because we happen to disapprove of totemism or human sacrifice as it would be to deny the reality of his hunger because we are offended at his table-manners. Man's religious instinct is as much a part of his essential equipment as is his fear, his love, or his gang sense, and he is as unlikely to 'grow out' of the first, through the development of civilisation, as he is to discard the others. Any parents who ignore their children's religious sense are in as great a peril of harming them as if they ignored any other item of their emotional life.

The next thing to observe about this primitive religious sense is that it began, like other human instincts and emotions, as a communal affair—it grew out of the 'gang'. Just as man's self-consciousness grew out of, and was shaped in the matrix of, his gang-consciousness, so his sense of personal religion grew out of the gang-religion. This, it is worth noting, runs somewhat counter to the general trend of Christian thought, especially since the Reformation; many people have got the idea firmly into their heads that religion is essentially a personal thing—a matter primarily for the individual soul—and that it has to be extended later to the fellowship of the group—to the family, the Church, the nation, and the world. I am far from denying the validity or necessity of this individual experience for the fully-developed 'new brain' man; all I am concerned with at the moment is to point out that, historically, this is a reversal of the natural order. Man's first 'experience' of religion was a communal rather than an individual affair.

If this be accepted its importance as regards the family gang is obvious. It means that if we are going to work along natural lines our children's first introduction to religion must also be a gang affair—it must be a matter of 'we' and 'us', not of 'I' and 'you'. The same principles of co-operation fostered through leadership which should guide the new family gang in its social development must also govern its religious growth, otherwise that growth will not be along healthy and natural lines. The children are made to grow that way in religion, as they are in society. This, of course, is where Mr. Barrett of Wimpole Street—or his religious-minded counterparts—went wrong; they regarded religion as something to be taught to the children and imposed on them rather than as a gang activity, that is, something to be learnt *with* the children and explored collectively.

I am well aware that in this second section of this book I shall be catering for a smaller public than in the first. There may be many who would be prepared to agree, on the whole, with what I have said about the family gang in general who will not be prepared to admit that religion should have any place in the modern set-up. To such people I can do no more than bid a regretful adieu; this is not the place for religious apologetic and I can only point out to them what I have already remarked, that the religious instinct is one of the most fundamental of man's primitive inheritances and that they will ignore it in their children at the peril of doing violence to the 'old brain'. It is my own belief, on the other hand, that religion, rightly apprehended, is the most powerful of all the influences that can mould the new family gang and enable its members to become good citizens of the complex new-brain societies. In the economy of Heaven-on-Thames the Heaven is quite as important as the Thames.

But even those parents who need no convincing—or are ready to be convinced—of the importance of religion in the family are often, in these modern days, filled with doubt and perplexity as to how religious teaching should be given. There is a whole host of awkward questions people are asking themselves about the subject, and some of them are very difficult for the plain man or woman to answer. For one thing, is it right to give definite religious teaching to young children? We are aware that many new educational theories are in the air, theories about giving children freedom and not attempting to thrust things down their throats too young, and leaving them to find things out for themselves. Is it right to give them ideas about religion in the nursery stage? Then again, we know—many of us, perhaps, somewhat vaguely—that a great mass of scientific work has been done on the Bible in recent years by the experts and that some of the ideas and beliefs held firmly by our grand-parents have been modified or even disproved. We do not want to teach our children anything which they may have to unlearn when they grow older. Moreover, there is all this modern talk about child psychology. The job of teaching young children is becoming more and more, we feel, a job for highly-trained experts, and we hear horrifying tales of the damage that may be done to children's minds by wrong treatment. Perhaps we have memories of our own childhood days when some well-meaning but wrong-headed grown-up tried to force instruction on us against our will and inclination, with the result that some particular subject has been distasteful to us ever since. We don't want to make that particular mistake with our own children; religion, we feel, is so desperately important that it would be a tragedy if we put them off it by unwise forcing. And finally, many of us simply do not know how to tackle the job, even though we may be convinced of its necessity. Our knowledge, both of children and of religion, is inadequate for the task, and we are afraid of doing harm. So it is hardly surprising that many people end up by doing nothing about it at all, leaving it to the schools and churches.

Before I attempt to deal with some of these perplexities and to suggest ways in which the family gang adventure in religion may be undertaken I must clear the ground by saying something about the parents upon whom the task of leadership will devolve. They may be divided, roughly speaking, into four classes. First there are those—I have already referred to them—who simply have no use for religion at all, in any form, and do not want their children to have any use for it either. They think—if they think about it at all—that religion is nothing but a lot of superstitious nonsense which is rapidly being de-bunked by science, and that the sooner the world discards it and gets down to reality, or brass tacks, or whatever they call it, the better. I do not suppose that anything I shall say in these pages will carry any weight with these people, and it is no part of my purpose, as I have already said, to attempt any apologetic for the truth of religion. But I would again point out to them that the religious instinct is one of the fundamental primitive inheritances of man and is, therefore, natural to children. I know that it is not obvious in many of them, but I am convinced, from thirty years' close observation, that it is inherent in them all. Historically, I imagine, the growth of the religious instinct in primitive man was very closely allied with the development of his fears. This may be a disquieting thought to the protagonists of present-day religion, but it is one which has to be faced squarely. The truth of the matter is that we moderns have gone badly wrong over this question of fear, we have degraded into the position of a contemptible vice that which was—and ought still to be—a most valuable item in man's emotional equipment. The primitive man's fear grew wholly out of his sense of reality—Nature *was* to be feared, and he could not come to terms with her or achieve a successful life with her if he did not learn to fear her, and to fear her very heartily and thoroughly. The primitive man's fear was, of course, in many ways much more objective than is that of his modern representative—and this, I fancy, is one of the sources of our trouble. The wolf, cave-bear, and sabre-tooth tiger *were* to be feared extremely, and there were plenty more of Nature's little unpleasantnesses in those days to re-inforce the lesson, if re-inforcement were needed. But man's fears did not spring entirely from those natural enemies which warred against him, it grew also out of his consciousness of the vastness and the terror of the natural world. It grew with his growing self-consciousness which must have impressed him continually with his own smallness and weakness. Nature is splendid as well as terrible, adorable as well as fearable, but it may well have been that the sense of terror preceded the sense of grandeur and that man learned, by bitter experience, to fear Nature before he learned to love her. However this may be, I believe it to be true that *primitive religion was, in the first place, primitive man's solution of the problem of fear.* As his consciousness and reasoning power developed this solution took two forms, the forms of god and devil. Man, with his itch to objectivise everything, embodied his vague fears in the person of a devil or evil spirit, something he could deal with on the plane of every-day reality by fighting it or at least placating it. Perhaps it was later in his development that the glory and wonder of Nature drove him to conceive of a god on whose friendly protection he could rely; but both—whether god or devil—were fundamentally an answer to the problem of fear. This suggestion may, at first glance, seem to suggest the truth of the German philosopher's gibe that 'Man created God in his own image', that religion is a purely subjective affair and has no counterpart in reality; but a moment's thought will show that this is far from being the case. Your little boy may wake in the dark, be overcome by fantastic fears, and stretch his arm across the bed in panic for his mother. The fears themselves may be 'mythical', but that does not prove that mother is a myth; it may have been fear that first drove primitive man to seek for God, but the really significant fact is that he found Him, and when he did find Him he discovered that God was not only the answer to the problem of fear, He was also the answer to the problem of love. The glory, as well as the terror, of Nature was accounted for.

I suggest, tentatively, that this close connection, on the deeper instinctive levels, between fear and religion may have something to do with the disfavour into which religion has fallen in modern times and be responsible for a good deal of so-called atheism. For fear is no longer regarded as a respectable instinct, it is not recognised as a necessary part of man's emotional equipment and—since it is in fact a part of our equipment whether we like it or not—this means that it is repressed. And if fear is repressed the answer to fear—religion—is naturally repressed too. The truth is that we all have a haunted wing in the mansion of our soul and that too many of us take the short cut of shutting up the haunted rooms and pretending that they do not exist. This is just another case of that ' cutting of the wires ' between the old brain and the new to which I referred in an earlier chapter, and it never results in true health. We must remember that the chapel of our soul is also situated in the haunted wing, and that if we run away from our ghosts we shall also run away from God. One of the greatest needs of modern society is that fear should be restored to respectability.

This digression on the subject of fear has led me away from my immediate subject, but the matter is of such outstanding importance as it affects the children in the family gang that I make no apology. Paradoxical as it may sound, one of the troubles that afflict modern children is that they have not enough to be afraid of. Life—all their immediate surroundings—has become so safe for them that there are no longer enough natural outlets for their inherited—and quite ineradicable—fear instinct. One of the results of this is the problem child who is ' a mass of fears '—the fear instinct has turned inwards and has become that most terrible of all afflictions the fear of life itself. They are afraid of life partly because they no longer have the sabre-tooth tiger to provide a healthy outlet for their emotion. We have no time here to enter deeply into questions of child psychology, but I would urge all parents who intend to embark on the family gang adventure to take their children's fears seriously. The first thing to recognise is that they are a genuine and quite natural part of every child's equipment and that they are nothing to be ashamed of. The second principle must be that fear is always something to be used, not something to be repressed; our job is not to teach the children not to fear, but to teach them what to fear. The third aim must be to 'objectivise' fear as far as possible, to transform it from being vague and shadowy to being something concrete; it is much healthier for your child to be afraid of cows than to be afraid of life. Only when they are objectivised in this way can the fears be faced and dealt with, the ghosts must be enticed from the haunted wing and installed in the drawing room—or better still in the workshop. That was how primitive man dealt with the sabre-tooth tiger which intimidated him, he may have run away to begin with but ultimately he learned to set a trap for him and in the end he feasted on his dead body. That is the principle you must have in mind always when dealing with your children's fears, every fear must be regarded, from a long-term point of view, as potentially the main dish for a picnic. And finally don't be too keen in discouraging your children from running away—it is one of the purposes for which God provided them with legs, and it is sometimes the best possible way of using them. One of the things which civilisation will have to re-learn when it restores fear to its proper place is the noble and ancient art of running away.

The second class of parents is composed of those who look upon religion as a useful accomplishment, a mark of refinement and respectability, a sign of good form, something which all boys and girls ought to 'acquire'—in strict moderation—during the course of their education. They ought to be baptised and confirmed just as they should have their tonsils out and their eyes tested, they should go occasionally to church just as they should go now and then to the dentist. Besides, these people say, a little religion is a steadying influence and may prevent the youngsters from doing anything silly or extravagant; children need a little religion just as they need a little codliver-oil—it helps to build them up.

I doubt, again, whether anything I shall say here will be of much use to these particular parents. Although I do not share their estimate of religion I think they are right about one thing— religion does have a steadying effect on those who come under its influence, whether they be old or young. Facing reality always steadies us, particularly if the reality is something big and splendid and inspiring and mysterious—something which appeals to both the old brain and the new. But is this conventional top-dressing kind of religion 'reality'—is it religion at all? I doubt it; at any rate I am sure that these people are wrong in one fundamental respect, religion—real religion—is not concerned in the least with conventional respectability or good form or anything like that, the verdict of history is quite definite on that point. Christianity certainly has never stood for that kind of respectability—not real living Christianity. It was born in persecution and nurtured in ridicule, its hall-mark is a felon's gallows, and whenever it has broken out afresh in all its living power—as it has a thousand times throughout the ages, both within the Church and outside it—persecution and ridicule have followed almost automatically. There is always something revolutionary about real religion, it turns men and women inside out and it tends to turn the world upside down. You can play with pretty conventions, but you cannot play with real religion, it is too dangerous. If you try it, you will find that you are playing with fire, and fire, even if it be the heavenly fire, is apt to burn. Jesus of Nazareth is no Leader for those who want to play for safety and who put the highest value on conventions. I stress this point because we parents must realise—and it is another fact to be faced squarely at the start—that if we set out to bring real religion into our homes we are setting out on an adventure that may well be dangerous. We shall be teaching our children to play with fire, and we as well as they may get burned.

The third class, and I am sure that it is a large one, contains those who really are deeply and passionately convinced of the power and reality of religion, whether by upbringing or by personal conviction or both, and are genuinely concerned to pass on their faith to their children, but are perplexed as to how it is to be done. Some of them, perhaps, retain vivid memories of their own upbringing in a religious home of the last generation, memories of family prayers and very emphatic dogmatic teaching—some of it rather grim and terrifying—and Sunday restrictions, and so on. They are thankfully conscious of the enormous debt they owe to this upbringing, of the power and direction it has given to their lives, and yet they are equally aware that it was not *all* good, some of the childish pictures they formed then in their minds of God and the moral order were crude and wrong and stultifying. And what an extraordinary power of endurance these childish pictures possess ! We think we have grown out of them or beyond them, and yet we find them re-appearing again and again on the background of our mind like the blood-stain in the ghost story. We cannot get rid of them, they condition our thinking against our will. It is often a terribly hard matter, when one becomes a man, to put away childish things. So these parents, conscious of the defects as well as the value of their own upbringing, are desperately anxious not to give their own children wrong notions of God and of religion which may handicap them in their turn. How is the gold to be handed on without the dross ? No wonder they are perplexed.

The fourth class contains those who are not themselves consciously religious—very possibly they call themselves agnostics—and yet have come to the conclusion that they would like their children, if possible, to acquire a faith which they themselves have missed. It may have been the bitter experience of life which has driven them to this conclusion, and I have no doubt that these terrible years of war have added a good many recruits to this class. Materialism and reasonableness and common sense, backed up by science and psychology and all the other 'ologies which the new brain has produced, have failed to make the world a really good place for men and women—and children—to live in. Reasonableness and common sense are simply not strong enough to cope with the evil and madness in the world. Perhaps there may be some bitter personal experience behind it too. Perhaps they have found that there is a power of evil within themselves, something which corrupts and distorts and maims, something which has spoiled life for them in spite of all the common sense and scientific knowledge and will-power they have tried to bring to bear on it. They are disillusioned, these people, and apt to be cynical, and they are often very, very tired. They do not believe in any of the creeds and in any case it is too late, they think, for them to change, but they do want their children to get hold of something better—something which will help them to face the world and society and their own temperaments with a bit more chance of success. But how are they to do it ? They know well enough that it is just silly wishful thinking to expect children to learn, or to catch, true religion from school or church if it is absent from the home atmosphere. And yet how in the world are these parents to teach or hand on to their childen something which they themselves do not possess ? That is their problem.

It is with these last two classes of parents in mind that I want to discuss in the following pages some of the problems of religion in the family gang. We shall do so, I hope, in the firm and confident conviction that the family is now, and must always be in the future, the most important and the most necessary social group in the world—the only natural group in which children can learn to be citizens of either Heaven-on-Thames or Heaven-hereafter. We shall refuse to be intimidated by the family theories of either Comrade Lenin or Mr. Barrett of Wimpole Street, though we shall be ready to learn from both. We shall keep firmly in mind the rock from which we are all hewn—the primitive family gang—but we shall have no less clearly in view the goal to which we are bound, a Heaven-on-Thames which is capable of an expansion to embrace Heaven-on-Seine and Heaven-on-Spree and Heaven-on-Volga, as well as all the other Heavens on

Earth. And we shall remember, with equal confidence, that the religious instinct is as much part of our children's inborn equipment as is any other of their emotions; rightly apprehended it is at once the greatest solvent and the most powerful cement at our disposal, for religion binds communities together more strongly than any other bond and it is, as it has always been, the solution of the problem of fear.

CHAPTER 6

MINDS AND WORDS

It has often been said—it has become indeed almost a religious wise-crack—that religion cannot be taught, it can only be caught. This may be true enough, but it does not bring much comfort to most of us; however conscious we may be of our unfitness to teach religion to children we are probably even more aware of our inability to hand it on to them by infection—they won't catch much, we feel, if they have to catch it from us. But there is a third possibility; if religion cannot be taught—and that is only a half-truth after all, for teaching is necessary and good teaching may be effective—and cannot be caught from us, it may be *sought* by ourselves and the children together, according to the time-honoured principles of the true family gang. And I believe that the family gang—father and mother and children working in equal partnership—is the best of all groups for such a search. It must be a democratic expedition if it is to succeed, there must be no laying down the law or heavy stuff of the kind dear to our friend Mr. Barrett; each member of the crew will bring his or her special contribution, the seniors their experience and intellectual power, the juniors their imagination and their direct vision—that priceless possession of childhood—together with their uncompromising realism.

The responsibility for planning and equipping and launching this expedition will obviously rest upon the parents, not the children, and this is going to entail for them a deal of hard work, careful thought, and detailed planning. Moreover, families are usually small in these degenerate days and there will certainly not be room in the family boat for any passengers lolling idly on the cushions and reading newspapers, or taking a merely bored, tolerant view of the proceedings. You may have to carry some of the children with you at first by a certain amount of cajolery and suggestion, but if either of the senior members is there under protest, or is not in earnest, then the expedition is doomed to failure. There need be no dishonesty or sham about this; perhaps one—or even both—of the senior members may have to say quite frankly "This is all new to me. I've never thought much about religion before, and I'll have to start from scratch, right from the A.B.C. I'm afraid I can't take the helm—I don't know enough about the job—you'll have to make me cabin-boy!" That is perfectly all right provided that he or she is game to *be* the cabin-boy and take the job seriously; there is no room for passengers. And remember, the gang is pledged to seek and to find the real thing, not a sham. The conventional, tame, wishy-washy, top-dressing, codliver-oil type of religion is not worth seeking—or finding. This is to be a flat-out adventure, a spiritual D-day, and there is to be no turning back. There may be storms and the risk of ship-wreck ahead and Heaven knows where we shall land up, but we are going through with it—to the end. That decision has got to be made, crystal-clear, before we set out.

At this point, I ought, perhaps, to say a word to forestall a criticism which may be in the minds of some readers. They may feel that I am being far too individualistic and free-lance over this matter of the family search for religion; what about the authority and teaching of the Church and of her Ministers? Is each individual family, then, to be a law unto itself, sailing its own course guided alone by its own whims and fancies, regardless of the experience of others? Of course not, that would be folly. I shall have more to say about the Church and its vital part in our venture as I go on. We are not sailing, after all, in uncharted seas and we must take with us—and use—the charts which have been prepared by those navigators who have ventured before us. We shall need the advice and direction of experts in this voyage, and we shall be no better than fools if we neglect them. Moreover, before we have gone very far we shall discover that we are not alone in these seas, there is a flotilla of other little craft around us, bound on the same quest. We may even find ourselves in a convoy and it may be wise policy to take orders from the escort-ships. There are many different convoys in this divided Christendom of ours, and they do not all follow the same route. It may ultimately be necessary for us to leave one convoy and join another, or even to sail for a time alone, though I hope not for long, since real religion is a vitally social thing and fellowship—wide and deep fellowship—is an essential part of it, as we shall find soon enough. And fellowship means at least some organisation, and organisation means discipline, and discipline means obedience. The City of God is a city, not a hamlet, and Heaven-on-Thames must be a city too. We are no longer primitive solitary hunters in the primeval jungle, either materially or spiritually.

I want to deal, for the remainder of this chapter, with one of the most important pieces of equipment with which we seniors must provide ourselves before we set forth on the family gang adventure in search of God. We must have at any rate some understanding of the way a child's mind works and of the best way to appeal to it, and the starting-point for this understanding must be a certain attitude of our own minds. The late George Hamilton Archibald, the Sunday School reformer, who had more wise things to say about children than anyone I have ever met, used one phrase again and again in his lectures; "Adultism is the bane of Childhood." Adultists—if I may coin the word—are people who think that children are simply adults on a small scale with primitive adult minds and elementary adult ideas. They are very fond of using such phrases as "explained in simple words that even a child can understand"; when you come across an expression of that kind in print you may be tolerably certain that it was written by an adultist. Adultists are fond of saying and of thinking that they 'understand children,' but the real trouble with them is that they do not understand themselves. They are always producing books and talks that are 'written down' for children—that is their strong suit, writing down and talking down to the young. These adultists are occupying a pinnacle of superiority all the time; they regard children, quite unconsciously, as an inferior order of grown-ups—inferior, inexperienced, undeveloped little adults. One of my earliest memories is of an old-fashioned though devoted nannie allowing me, as a birthday treat, to partake of the cake after she had picked out the currants. That is the typical adultist attitude to children's fare, both material and spiritual; it must be watered down and simplified, with the kick taken out of it—cake without the currants, life without the tragedy, Christianity without the Crucifixion.

Now this adultist attitude, with its conceit on the one hand and its ignorance of the fierce realism and courage of the children on the other, is pernicious nonsense, and the first thing we adult members of the crew must do is to throw it overboard for good and all. It is one of the worst of our legacies from Mr. Barrett of Wimpole Street, and there is no place for it in the new family gang. For whatever a small boy may be he is most certainly not a little man, nor is a young girl a little woman. Their minds are different from ours not only in degree but in kind; in some ways they are superior to ours, and it is important that we should recognise the fact. Earlier in this chapter, when speaking of the children, I referred to their 'direct vision' and 'uncompromising realism'; those are two of the respects in which they are often superior to us—they see some things more quickly, more clearly, and more realistically, and they can often show us the way. Moreover I believe that young children are often in direct, though unconscious, touch with ultimate reality much more closely than are their elders, their minds have not yet acquired the padding of civilisation. They cannot talk about it and of course they cannot explain it, but it gives a certain quality to their thinking which we older people have largely lost. This is not sentimentality, it is simple hard fact. One of the best bits of preparation the senior members of the crew can undertake is to read through carefully—and more than once—Wordsworth's 'Ode on the Intimations of Immortality,' for besides being magnificent poetry this contains some of the soundest horse sense that has ever been written on the subject of children. Unless we are prepared to recognise the unique qualities of children, to reverence them and learn from them and sometimes be guided by them, this business of building up a family religious life will be a failure. Overboard, then, with adultism! The adultist's slogan, though of course he would never admit it, is "Unless the children are changed and become like us adults they will not enter the Kingdom of Heaven"; Jesus of Nazareth, you may remember, said the exact opposite, and He knew what He was talking about.

It is, however, perfectly true that the children's minds are immature and undeveloped, and we must understand their limitations as well as their virtues before we tackle the job of teaching them. One of the most important of these limitations—and one that closely concerns our present adventure—is that children have little or no capacity to understand abstractions or generalisations. We adults are constantly using words and expressions whose meaning has been built up in our minds by a slow accumulation of spread-out experiences, such, for example, as the words 'warfare' or 'politics' or 'love.' Our idea of warfare is a generalisation made up from all that we know about fighting, past and present, and it takes a whole world of experience to get the hang of what is meant by politics. You cannot learn it from one example, or two, or three, it takes dozens and scores before you can generalise the mass of isolated impressions into a single unified idea; just seeing one parliamentary candidate kissing one baby will not teach you what politics mean. The same is true to an even greater extent about an even simpler word—love. *You* know well enough what it means, but it is a composite meaning built up from long observation of all kinds of love, both that experienced directly and that apprehended sympathetically through observation. But we must remember in all our dealings with them that children cannot generalise in this way because they lack the necessary experience, and that in consequence the meaning they will attach to such generalised words will be completely different from ours. Six-year-old Tommy will not know what you mean by warfare; he knows that he punched Billy Jones on the nose last Tuesday and that Billy punched him back, that he saw two boys fighting yesterday, and that he passed some soldiers marching in the street, but he cannot yet combine all these impressions and grasp warfare as a generalised idea, standing by itself. A moment's reflection will show us how tremendously this fact bears on the teaching of religion to children, and on the telling to them of Bible and other stories. The language of religion, like the language of the Bible, is adult language, full of just those abstractions and generalisations which the children are unable to grasp. It will not do them any harm to hear these used, but they will not know what they mean and we must not count on building anything on them. This is where the adultists fall down: they think that it is the simplicity of the language that matters, but they are wrong. The simplest of words, like the word 'love,' may be the most abstract of generalisations. We need to ask ourselves continually " What will Tommy understand by this word, or this phrase? What meaning will *he* give to it in the light of his experience up-to-date?"

This question of the meaning of words is so important that I want to devote a little more time to its consideration. I will illustrate it by two examples, the first of which happens to come from my own experience. When I was quite young—six or seven years old—my good aunt, who looked after us children, used to take me on Sundays to the Parish Church, where it was sometimes my lot to hear the Litany read. The Parson read out a list of terrible dangers—most of which I did not understand, though they gave me a vague impression of menace and horror—and then the congregation all round me said, again and again, the words " Good Lord, deliver us." I knew what they meant by " Good Lord "—they were speaking to God—and I also thought that I knew what they meant by " deliver," a word which was used, in much the same way, in the Lord's Prayer. Oh yes, I knew what " deliver " meant all right; two or three times a week I trotted with my aunt down to the village to do the household shopping, and didn't we go to the Grocer—I can smell the actual aroma of his shop as I write—and didn't he always say, when the order had been given, " We'll deliver these without fail this afternoon, Madam?" And didn't I know the bright green Grocer's van, always drawn by an old grey horse, which duly drove up to our house in the afternoon? And when the door at the back of the van had been opened and the driver was carrying the parcels into the kitchen, hadn't I often crept inside and squatted down in the interior among the racks of parcels with their fascinating smells of coffee and cheese and bacon ? Of course I knew what " deliver " meant ! The people in Church were asking God to pop them safely into a bright green van when they were in trouble and to drive them off to Heaven behind an old grey horse ! And a very sensible request too, I thought; what better way out of trouble could you want than to be packed into that lovely van among all those delicious things to eat, and to be driven away to safety by God ? I thought of Him, needless to say, as the driver of the van, dressed in His clean white coat. And to this day, I must confess, I can never hear those words in Church without the picture of a bright green van and an old grey horse coming, quite unbidden, before my eyes.

I am sure that this is typical of what is happening to tens of thousands of children every day, at home and at school, and particularly in the sphere of religion. They are getting hold of wrong or distorted ideas which may permanently affect their thinking simply because they are giving the wrong meaning to words. And remember, the language of religion is especially full of words and phrases which are either abstract or, like my word ' deliver,' have more than one meaning. Before you read the Bible to children, or tell them a Bible story, or pray with them, you must go through your language literally word by word, asking yourself " What will Jimmy and Mary understand by this ? What meaning will they give to it ? " There is no general answer to that question, no answer you can get out of a text-book or a treatise on child psychology; no two children have had quite the same experience and no two will give quite the same meaning to any words—and they form the majority of our vocabulary of nouns and adjectives—which require experience for their interpretation. Only you, who know the children intimately, can get at their minds—and even you will slip up often enough !

Then again, besides these words like ' deliver ' which children may get wrong by accident, as it were, but may understand quite well after a brief explanation, there are other words which they cannot understand at all, in the adult sense, because of their lack of experience. That all-important word ' love ' is one of these, and my second example deals with that very point. Johnny, aged six, was an only child. For a few weeks his cousin Percy, of the same age, had been staying with him to get away from the bombs, and naturally Johnny's parents had done their best to be kind and affectionate to the little evacuee. Johnny had resented this bitterly; he didn't in the least like sharing his parents with an outsider and was furiously jealous of his cousin. Then one night mother was telling Johnny about Jesus and the little children and finished up—as grown-ups are apt to do—with some such remark as " So you see, Johnny, Jesus loves *all* the children in the world, just like that, and of course he loves *you* ! " A frown came over Johnny's face at that, and he scowled for a moment in silence. Then he burst out with "Does Jesus love *Percy*, Mummy ? " " Yes, of course he does ! " said Mummy, rather pleased that her son had raised the point and hoping that the moral might go home. " Then I *hate* Jesus, I *hate* him ! I won't be loved by him ! " shouted Johnny defiantly, and marched off to bed with his hands in his pockets, whistling. Poor mother, of course, was shattered. " How naughty of Johnny ! " she sighed— and yet, you know, it was entirely her own fault, she had not thought out beforehand what she was saying. And what was wrong ? Why, simply that Johnny's idea of love was quite different from her own, that was all. A young child's notion of love is derived, as a rule, from one source and one set of experiences only—his relationship to his mother, with father as a kind of extension in the background. This love is very possessive, intensely personal, and in one sense almost wholly selfish in that it is the product of dependence, it has grown out of receiving everything, not giving. Moreover it is, quite naturally and rightly, exclusive—that, of course, was what was wrong with Johnny. He was not ready, yet, for any generalisation of the idea of love, and mother, being aware of his feelings towards Percy, ought to have known it. I am sure, myself, that it is a mistake to generalise the idea of love, and of other emotions, with young children. I should avoid as far as possible the use of such phrases as " The Love of God " or " The Love of Jesus " in any universal sense, the children do not, and cannot, know what they mean and they may be put off by them or get quite wrong and inadequate ideas. They can grasp the concrete instances all right, just as Tommy, who did not know what warfare meant, had a very vivid memory of punching Billy Jones on the nose. I am sure that the right line with children is to give them any number of concrete instances, as vivid and personal as you can make them, and to leave them to work out the generalisations for themselves as they become able to do it. But we must not on any account try to do it for them, or to point the moral; if we do we shall only put them off, like young Johnny.

All this may sound somewhat alarming and complicated, but in actual fact it is going to make our work much simpler. It means that the 'religious instruction' given in the family gang will be given almost wholly, to begin with, through the medium of stories. And in the Bible as a whole and the Gospels in particular we have a perfect mine of just these very concrete instances for which we are seeking. If we are not going to talk, for the time being, about the love of Jesus for mankind we can tell the stories of His care for the leper by the roadside, the little daughter of Jairus, the nobleman's son, blind Bartimaeus, Zacchaeus the tax-collector, and a dozen others. The children will put two and two together and will make the generalisation in their own good time.

CHAPTER 7

STORIES

In the last chapter I discussed the important business of telling stories to children, with particular reference to the problem presented to the story-teller by the children's inability to understand generalised words. I am convinced, myself, that very nearly all the actual religious teaching in the family gang should be done through the medium of stories. You cannot, of course, present the whole of religion in that particular way, but we are not concerned with the whole, we are dealing with foundations—the foundations which can be laid in the family and nowhere else. The superstructure—the completed edifice—will not be the work of the family gang only, it will be the result of a combined operation by family, Church, and individual, with all the social and intellectual influences of Heaven-on-Thames taking their part. But the family gang is the best place in the world for story-telling, and since it is our purpose to help the children to learn the art of generalisation from numbers of particular instances our main vehicle of teaching will be the story.

You often hear people say "I am no good at story-telling," and they are probably perfectly correct. The art does not find a place in the curriculum of any secondary or technical school and is not included in the syllabus of those seminaries of domestic science which set out to prepare young women for the task of running a home. Yet the ability to tell stories, and to tell them well, is quite as important in the family economy as is the ability to cook and, like cooking, it is an art that can be learned. The two essentials for it are a lively imagination and a sense of drama, and though both of these have been titillated by the modern vogue of the cinema their exercise, as creative activities of the mind, has just as surely been atrophied. This, of course, is the result of civilisation, and it is true of many human faculties besides the two I have just mentioned. Our pleasure in a work of art or imagination was intended by Nature to be inseparable from our pleasure in the act of creation; we were all intended to be craftsmen as well as customers, artists as well as critics. The result of machinery, in all its forms, mental as well as material, has been to short-circuit the creative part and confine the whole of our pleasure to the possessive element, the enjoyment we experience in the finished article. Whenever we habitually become accustomed to something being done for us, whether it be our food which is pre-digested or our emotion pre-fabricated in Holywood, we tend to lose the faculty of doing it for ourselves and the pleasure of enjoyment becomes divorced from the joy of creation. There is no need to mourn unduly over this change or to languish miserably for the good old days, but we must recognise the trend and allow for it, using the wits of our new brain to restore the balance of the old. Heaven-on-Thames, I would venture to prophesy, will be full of dramatic societies, art clubs, and craft guilds, though it is possible that ration-books may be issued for the cinema. Shakespeare and Shaw will still be acted, even if many of the other plays are both home-made and home-produced, and Old Masters will still hang in the municipal picture-gallery alongside the rooms which will be reserved, month by month, for the paintings and drawings of the school-children. The new society must re-discover for its rank and file the joy of creation, for it is only healthy creation that makes possible sane criticism.

All this is something of a digression, but it is very relevant to this business of story-telling. The stories in the Gospels are cut to the bone as regards detail and dramatic development, the bare facts are given in the fewest possible words, and if they are to be re-created for the children so that they may come alive and touch them on the level of their own experience they must be re-clothed with all the imaginative art and dramatic power that the teller has at his disposal.

As a preliminary to this undertaking I suggest that the would-be story teller should buy a special copy of the Gospels and read them carefully through, marking in the margin those passages and incidents which he thinks would work up into suitable stories.

The references of these passages may also be entered in a note-book and a subject-heading supplied for each. An examination of the material so obtained will be enough, I expect, to impress on the most optimistic something of the magnitude and difficulty of the task that lies before him. But before he attempts it there is an important question to be settled about the form which the stories shall take. There are, I think, three possible alternatives. The first is to eschew all adornments and additions of any description and simply to read the stories in the words of the Bible itself, either the Authorised Version or one of the modern translations. This method, though it will appeal to some as preserving the sacred authority of Scripture and to others as saving trouble, has two grave drawbacks; the strangeness of the words and phrases of Bible language, and the extreme terseness of the narratives themselves, many of which are compressed into the compass of no more than a dozen lines. With the first of these difficulties I have already dealt, but the second is an even more serious drawback; if stories are to be told effectively to children they must be cast in a certain form and obey certain rules, none of which are present in the Gospel narratives. The Gospels are not full-length biographies, they are condensed summaries, expressed in the fewest possible words. Their writers were not aiming to 'tell a story' but to record facts.

The second method is to 'mug up', in the schoolboy phrase, a vast amount of detail about life in Palestine in the first century of our era, facts about food and clothing and organisation and social habits and climate and a hundred other matters, and then to expand the stories with the material so collected, endeavouring to keep strictly to what is 'true' or at any rate 'likely' in the local colour and detail. There is much to be said for this method, particularly if the children concerned have lively and intelligent minds. It will be a real piece of genuine education—for the parents as much as for the children—and, if well done, it will give every-body an insight into the life of a semi-oriental people of two thousand years ago which will be a valuable asset for the whole of their lives. There are again, however, certain drawbacks which must be taken into account as well as the advantages. In the first place it is not all parents who have the time, the facilities, or the mental equipment for the historical study which is involved, and in the second place the whole effect of such a treatment will be to remove the stories from the living present to the dead and remote past. They will be the stories of very far away and of very long ago. The more thoroughly and intelligently the work is done the more obvious will it be that things were different then and the easier it will be to feel that the meaning, as well as the setting, of the stories is something far removed from present-day life. Moreover, the differences of setting will need constant explanation if misunderstandings are to be avoided, and nothing spoils the flow of a story more than interruptions of that character.

The third method is to regard the stories as belonging to eternity, not to time, and to tell them frankly in as modern a setting as possible, with many of the properties of the stage of today. This is the method of Shakespeare, and of the mediaeval miracle plays, and it has stood the test of both time and experience. Shakespeare did not hesitate to put his ancient Britons and Roman Senators alike into the buskins of the Elizabethan age nor to fill their minds and mouths with the thoughts and words of his own time; while the mediaeval Church staged the drama of the Christian story in the costumes of the moment, dressing the Queen of Heaven in the latest Paris fashion and arming the devils of Hell with all the instruments of the most up-to-date feudal torture-chamber. And the people who watched, whether they adored or whether they trembled, were loving or fearing something which belonged to the 'now' of life up-to-the-minute.

This third method is not, of course, without difficulties and dangers of its own. Many people doubt the wisdom and rightness of telling Bible stories to children with a lot of imaginary detail added, a good deal of it probably inappropriate to the real Gospel setting. "Bye-and-bye" they say "the children will read the original account, and then they will feel that they have been deceived, and you will lose their confidence." This is a real danger, and you must guard against it. By far the best way of doing this is to make the stories, right from the beginning, a co-operative effort in which every member of the family takes his or her part. Suppose, for instance, you are telling them the story of Jairus's daughter as you find it in the fifth chapter of St. Mark. The little girl's name is not mentioned, so she must be given one, and the children can supply it. " I'm going to tell you a story about a little girl, but I don't know her name—what shall we call her ? " And again—" She had been ill, so I expect she had her toys with her in the room, put aside on the table. What toys do you think she had ? " And later, when Jesus tells the parents to give her something to eat—" What do you suppose they gave her ? " Tommy may vote for sausage-and-mash and perhaps Betty will suggest an ice. " So Mother, when she had finished hugging her, just *ran* into the kitchen and got ready the most delicious sausage-and-mash you ever saw, with a strawberry ice to follow ! " Of course it is make-up, but if the children have provided a good deal of the make-up themselves, as a piece of co-operative gang effort, there will be no danger of any member confusing fact with fiction; they will understand the rules of the game and will not be puzzled or put off when they come to read, or to hear, the original tale in the words of the Authorised Version.

All your stories must be like this, detailed and vivid and full of local colour even if the tints be those of the twentieth rather than of the first century. If you are telling, for instance, the story of Jesus and the children, in the tenth chapter of St. Mark, do not say that a group of children were playing by the lake-side when Jesus came by—give them names, make them Tom and Mary and Joe and Naomi ; give them characters, too, and the other things that real children have such as grubby hands and snub noses and grazed knees and tousled heads. And make a real lake-shore, even if you have to get it from the pool in your city park. The children, of course, will want their favourite stories again and again—that is a most important part of the business—and you may be sure that you will get into trouble if you miss any bits out, especially the bits which the children themselves have contributed. "But, Mummy, you've forgotten the teddy-bear on the bed!" and "Mummy! She had an *ice* as well as a sausage!" We want the children to become familiar with the Bible words before long, but I am sure that it is wise policy to get them familiar with the actual story first; let them get the picture well into their heads—and remember that children think largely in pictures, not in words—and then link up the picture with the narrative as it is given in the New Testament. But let them link the Bible words on to a picture which they have already formed, if they get the Bible words first they may make the wrong pictures, for reasons I have already mentioned. As soon as the story is completed, rounded off and polished up and decorated with all the lively fancy and touches of humour which the gang can contribute to it, turn back to the original and let the gang read it together—"This is the piece from the Bible written down centuries ago by people who actually knew Jesus—out of which we have made our story." If you can follow this method successfully you will be giving the children, unconsciously, the right attitude to history, for history is no more than a few isolated facts standing out from a background of equally vital facts which have been forgotten or have gone unrecorded. We do not know any more, actually, about the Battle of Hastings or the death of the Princes in the Tower or the drama of Richard the Second and Wat Tyler than we do about the healing of Jairus's daughter. One of the commonest and most disastrous errors which ordinary school teaching implants in young minds is the idea that History—with a capital H—is what we know about the past. It is, of course, nothing of the kind—it is what actually happened, and that bears much the same relationship to the content of the text-books as the Piltdown Man, breathing, alive, and shaggy, bears to the fragment of bone which was found in the gravel of Sussex. History, like religion, can only be apprehended by the use of a lively and even daring imagination, and if true citizenship depends—as surely it does—on a true understanding of History, then the training and development of imagination to the highest degree must be one of the main educational tasks of Heaven-on-

Thames. War, with other hideous evils, is largely due to a failure of imagination; nobody whose imagination was really alive could either invent or use bombs and poison gas.

Your stories about the life of Christ, then, are to be recreated with the help of all the fancy and ingenuity which the family gang can bring to bear on them, and this is not going to be a mere concession to the ' weakness ' of the children, but a real training in the only true method of interpreting history. The preparation of these stories will be your main task for some time to come as senior partners in the family gang adventure in search of God, and you will need all the help you can get in a difficult and exacting task. The first obvious source of aid lies in books, particularly in those books—or such of them as are still available—which re-tell Bible stories for children. Like all other kinds of books some of these are good, some indifferent, and some bad, but from nearly all of them you can get some ideas and hints for your own story-telling. Some are illustrated and are intended for the children themselves to read; these are first-class when they are really well done, but be careful not to let the children's taste be corrupted by those sentimental, wishy-washy pictures—so dear to the ' adultists ' of whom I wrote in the last chapter—with their flaxen-haired simpering angels of children and their effeminate Christ. And however good the book-told stories may be, do not let them become a substitute for the home-made co-operative tale which is to be the peculiar possession—the personal craftsmanship—of your own family gang. Use the books as quarries or, if you prefer it, as a timber store, but not as a shop for the finished article. Your house, like the house in Nazareth, must contain a working-bench complete with tools, and the tools must be used by all.

The second source of aid lies in the wider fellowship of the Church, and here, right at the start, any unhealthy isolation of the family gang can be broken down. This business of home religious training has, on the whole, been sadly neglected by the churches; many of them are keen enough over their services, including their Children's Services and Sunday Schools, but how many of them have really laid themselves out to help the parents to give the vital home training which should be the foundation of Church membership ? This is not a thing that can be done by societies on a national scale, it is an individual matter concerning each small worshipping group by itself; it concerns the churches, not the Church. If there are two or three of you who read these pages—two or three connected with a particular worshipping group and determined to give this adventure a trial—why not get together and talk it over and then approach your parson and ask if he will help you ? There may be an experienced Sunday School worker available as well, and if the two should happen to belong to different communions, so much the better for the Church Universal of Christ on Earth. You might arrange a small discussion group, meeting occasionally in one another's houses with the Parson and Teacher present as experts; they will be able to advise you about the selection of the stories and their arrangement in a series and all the hundred-and-one points about language and interpretation and historical background which are their own special province. The parents composing such a group, on their part, would bring their own contribution springing from their direct contact with the children, and the more expert story-tellers among them would be able to share their ideas and explain their technique to the less skilled.

This brings me to the third source of reinforcement, a study of the art of story-telling in general, and that is so important a matter that it must have a chapter to itself.

CHAPTER 8

THE ART OF STORY-TELLING

The art of the raconteur is one of the oldest in the world and must have been developed in the primitive society which we considered in the first section of this book, along with that craft of stone-shaping which has given their names, among archaeologists, to the various primitive periods. Unfortunately it is only the stones which have survived: we would cheerfully give up a peck of the eoliths if we could recover one of the stories. However, even if we cannot recapture those tales of long ago we can make a fairly good guess, from our knowledge of present-day primitives, as to what they would be like. They would be in the main, probably, interminable yarns of exploits in the hunting field, illustrated with a wealth of miming action, in which the audience would doubtless find it tactful to join, particularly if the teller were a Nimrod of credit and renown. Sometimes, no doubt, the narrator would be a ' Club bore '—though the club might carry a different significance in those days—and then the reactions of his hearers would be perfunctory or negative, the little hunters round the edge of the camp-fire circle would wriggle and yawn just as yours and mine do when we strike an off-day in our yarning. But on other occasions it would be different: the eyes around the circle would light up with something more than the reflection of the flames, when the warrior seized his club to attack the bear in pantomime a dozen little hands would lay hold of sticks to wave in sympathy, and the dying howl of the wolf would be echoed shrilly from a dozen infant throats. The story in both cases might actually be the same, for primitive folk were as conservative in their tastes as any modern children and nobody would be allowed to take liberties with the traditional sagas of the gang, but its effectiveness would depend, then as now, on the genius of the story-teller. This is the first fact which the senior partners must realise at the outset of their adventure—everything depends on the story-teller. I have known a thrilling adventure-tale fall so flat that the tones of the speaker were almost drowned by the yawnings and shufflings of his hearers, and I have also known a common-place and almost pointless narration of a humdrum round of village shopping, told quietly by a certain old lady, so grip her restless audience that you could have heard a pin drop. It is not the story that matters so much, or even the technique of the telling—it is the teller himself. What is the secret of the art? It is, I think, in the main a matter of imaginative identification, the power to tell the simplest events as if they were the present experience of the narrator himself. No tale, however ancient, must be a twice-told tale, it must always be a new experience, told from the life. Strictly speaking you should never tell a story at all, you should only describe something real that you see happening before your eyes. Stories should not be re-told, they should be re-created, and re-creation, like creation, demands an artist. The narrator's power to grip his audience depends on the extent to which the tale he is telling has come alive in his own mind; the true story-teller must be one who is able to speak as seeing him who is invisible.

But we are not all geniuses and the great majority of us will have to rely on careful planning and skilful arrangement of material rather than on personal magnetism for the attainment of our object; there are certain principles which underlie all good story-telling and it will be well worth our while to study them.

The first point about a good story is that it should have a point, and when young children are involved it is almost equally important that it should not have more than one. Perhaps the commonest mistake that grown-ups make when they are teaching or story-telling to children is the mistake of trying to teach, or to tell, more than one thing at a time. "Firstly—secondly—thirdly" have no place in a children's sermon, and still less in the children's story; the young mind has only room in it for one idea at a time and the secondly will inevitably drive out the firstly while the thirdly will complete the ruin, expelling both its predecessors and itself. When you want to drive a stake into the hard ground you find it convenient to sharpen the stake into a single point; if you make two points the stake may enter a little way but it will soon refuse to make further progress and will tumble out of the hole at the lightest puff of the wind of distraction. If, on the other hand, it has a single point you may hammer it in, if you will, up to its head. If a children's story has two points, separate and distinct, it almost certainly contains the materials for two stories and should be divided accordingly. The narrator must discipline himself with the utmost sternness in the use of his material and resist the temptation, however seductive, to tell two stories or teach two lessons at the same time. If, when you are dealing with children, you try to kill two birds with one stone it is the children's interest which will be the casualty and both the birds will fly away to the tree-tops unscathed. The first thing to do, then, is to decide what is to be the point of the story and to shape its whole architecture so that that point, and that only, becomes its central feature to which every line and every detail leads up. If you fancy your story as a cathedral it is Salisbury or Saint Paul's you must copy—not Lichfield or Lincoln with their multiple towers and spires.

Having decided on the point of your story the next thing to do is to determine its shape, to plan it, that is, so that the point comes in the right place, which must obviously be very near to the end. Your edifice must after all be more like a parish church, with the spire at one end, than like Salisbury Cathedral with the steeple in the centre, if you are to avoid the tragedy of an anti-climax. In order to get an idea of the natural shape of the story it is often desirable—even if you are an expert story-teller already—to make a little diagram in advance, showing the 'line of interest'. The interest concerned is, of course, that in the mind of the hearer, not of the teller; you have to ask yourself what episodes in the tale the children will find exciting, or gripping, and what parts will be comparatively dull. When you have made your diagram you may find that it takes a shape somewhat resembling fig. 1., and in that case you will see at once that the architecture of the story is bad since the climax—the point of greatest interest—comes near the beginning and is bound to be followed by a drop in interest which will probably be associated with yawns and wrigglings. Fig. 1. represents, therefore, a thoroughly bad story. In fig. 2. the state of affairs is not quite so bad since for half the time the interest is steadily rising, but there is still too long a decline during the second half and even five minutes of declining interest may efface the impression produced by the climax. What, then, about fig. 3? Here the climax comes at the end and the impression made by it is more likely to be retained, but the form is not yet ideal since there is too long and too gradual a slope during the opening stages, and if the audience is a naturally restive one you may have difficulty in retaining its interest until you reach the mountain peak. What, then, are you to do about it? A very brief study of Grimm's Fairy Tales, or—better still—of the Arabian Nights, will provide the answer: the long upward slope to the ultimate mountain peak of interest must be enlivened, to keep the interest going, by a series of lesser peaks, so that the line of interest will take a form resembling that in fig. 4. The minds of the hearers are kept active and their interest is maintained by a series of minor crises leading up to the main climax which comes, as it must, right at the end of the story. And there is another point which is worth noting about fig. 4; you will observe that it begins, unlike its predecessors, at a fairly high level of interest. Anyone who had tried to begin a story to a large audience of restive children will know well enough the difficulty of catching their interest at the start, of establishing that point of contact which will induce the receptive mood. With many children, of course, this difficulty does not arise, they are anxious for a story, are looking forward to it, and the contact is easily made. But some are more kittle customers—as shy as trout—and expert casting is necessary before they can be securely hooked. Some experiences of mine when I was a young man rubbed this fact well into my mind. A group of us determined to make an effort to do something for the crowds of young people—many good folk would have called them hooligans—who at that time thronged the streets of Birmingham every Sunday night, marching aimlessly up and down to the accompaniment of much cat-calling and horseplay. We had no difficulty in persuading some two hundred of them to come into a big bare mission-room on the promise of some stories, but the problem was how to make a beginning through the deafening hubbub; forms were crashing over, half-a-dozen free fights were in progress, and in the front row one youth was brandishing a kitchen chopper in the manner of a tomahawk, to the accompaniment of ear-splitting Red Indian war-cries. The leader of our party, whose duty it was to tell the first story, watched the scene for a moment and then, snatching the chopper with a sudden quick movement, mounted the platform, and throwing back his head drew the edge of the chopper across his neck as if he were cutting his own throat. The noise ceased suddenly, and by the time he had repeated the movement there was a dead silence. " Not sharp enough " he said with a frown, feeling the edge of the chopper with his thumb. " And not half heavy enough ! But I'll tell you the story of a chopper as keen as a razor and heavy enough to sheer through a man's spine as if it were putty ! "—and before they knew what was happening they were listening to the tale of Damon and Pythias, with a silent absorption which would have filled Spurgeon himself with envy.

I do not suggest that your children should be classed with that unruly rabble or that you will have to fight so hard to get their attention, but the principle remains the same—that you should link, if you can, the beginning of your story on to something that belongs to the here and now of the children's consciousness.

When the story is told with an aim in view apart from entertainment—when, that is, it has a moral as well as a point—another complication arises in the architecture; where and how is the point to be introduced ? The answer is quite simple: In terms of our graphs, the point P, representing the instant when the 'lesson' is to be inculcated, must appear on the summit of the highest mountain; the story will be a failure, as far as its ultimate purpose is concerned, if it comes in a valley or on an upward or downward slope. This principle shatters at one blow the silly practice of 'pointing the moral' at the end of the story, so dear to the heart of most preachers. The gateway into the child's mind is open only for an instant, the instant of greatest excitement; the moral must get inside then or not at all, to attempt to introduce it as an afterthought, when the peak of interest is passing, is the equivalent—if the converse—of shutting the stable door after the horse has escaped. It is doubly foolish to point the moral at the end of a children's story, firstly because it is bound to be an anti-climax, and secondly because you are doing something *for* the children which they should—and must, if the impression is to remain—do for themselves. Jesus of Nazareth hardly ever pointed a moral; He seems to have preferred that his hearers should scratch their heads in complete bewilderment rather than enlighten them Himself. He knew that the effort of finding and applying the lesson was an absolutely vital factor in His hearers' apprehension of the truth; no one—not even He—could do that particular part of the business for them. His refusal to point the moral was not only the mark of a great story-teller, it was sound sense and sound psychology.

There is one more point we ought to notice about the art of story-telling before we pass on to other subjects, the point of pace and descriptive detail. These two hang closely together, for obviously the adding of descriptive detail must always slow up the speed of the narrative. When ought you to put in your detail, slowing up the story to do it, and when ought you to hurry along? You can get the answer quite easily if you make, and then study, your 'line of interest' diagram. When the line is *low*—when there is nothing happening that is particularly exciting or intriguing—hurry along quickly and avoid unnecessary detail; when you are on a peak of excitement you can slow up and 'prolong the agony' by putting in as much detail as you like. A study of the great stories of the world—I would recommend fairy stories and the Arabian Nights—will illustrate this again and again, and you will find the most successful writers of thrillers obeying the same rule. If, for example, I am telling a tale of mountaineering adventure and put in long descriptions of the sights seen by the mountaineer as he toils up the valley towards the peak my audience will soon become restive. But when the adventurer is hanging by a frayed rope over a thousand-foot precipice while his companion is inching his way along a nerve-racking ledge to rescue him I can pile on as much detail as I like.

"Just above his head he could see his own hands, clutching the rope, and he noticed inconsequently that one of his finger-nails was broken; hanging as he was on the very brink of death he felt an odd irritation that he could not get at his pen-knife and trim the offending nail. Following up the rope with his eyes he could see, just where it disappeared over the crag, that another strand had broken: three strands gone now, and still more strain on the rest! He knew there were twenty-four strands altogether—three gone, and twenty-one left—how long would they last? Beyond the crag, as his eyes strained upwards, he could see a great white cloud floating serenely over the mountain—the cloud needed no rope to hold it up there in the sky, why couldn't he float like a cloud . . . ? Ping! Another strand had gone . . . and then another. He felt the rope stretch with a sudden jerk. It wouldn't hold him much longer . . . what would it feel like to fall down . . . and down . . . and down . . . ? A mist came before his eyes and then, through it he saw the rough rock-wall of the mountain, a yard from his face. He gazed at the rock, fascinated. His eye followed up a little grey crack in the stone; he imagined himself an ant—a tiny man-ant trying to climb it. He looked at it critically, with the eye of the trained cragsman; what hand-holds and foot-holes would he use if he—an ant—had to climb that six-inch cranny? . . . . Ping! Another strand had gone—only eighteen left—John would never reach him in time, the rope couldn't hold for more than two minutes. Two minutes! A hundred and twenty seconds! His mind did the sum unconsciously—perhaps the last sum he would do in this world. His thoughts flashed homewards and he remembered, with a sudden irritation, that he had forgotten to buy the licence for Toby, his dog, before he had left home. He had to restrain himself from shouting to John to remind him about the licence . . . Ping! Another strand—seventeen left.

Then it would be sixteen—then fifteen . . ."

I do not pretend for a moment that this is good story-telling —it is common enough trash—but it does illustrate my point, that where the tension of excitement is great, there you can slow up the pace, make every second into an hour, and pile on the detail to your heart's content while the hair rises higher and higher on the heads of your spell-bound young hearers. And though the stories you tell together in the family gang when you are voyaging in search of religion may not be of quite so sensational a type the principle none the less holds good—put in your detail where the excitement is greatest.

You can learn other lessons, too, from the great story-tellers of the past. Note how the element of repetition comes in to give unity and force to the narrative. The three bears with their porridge-plates, each asking the same question one after another, the endless sets of three in the fairy-stories—three brothers, three sisters, three particular dangers or trials of strength which each encounters in a different way. All these are devices which give stability and coherence to the story, and you must be ready to make use of them in your own tales. If you are fortunate enough to be one of the natural geniuses in the art you may, of course, break all the rules and still get away with it, but the rules are worth studying none the less, for the old story-tellers were past-masters in the art and were wise in the ways of children—perhaps because they were not far from being children themselves.

Your task, then, will be to re-tell the Gospel stories with all the art and all the skill you can bring to them, re-creating them first in your own imagination, feeling them down to the tips of your toes, and telling them always as seeing Him who is invisible. You will not, of course, confine yourselves entirely to the Gospels, though they will always be the main stand-by, returned to again and again. The Old Testament is a perfect mine of magnificent stories, enough for a life-time. Many of them do, we must admit, raise certain moral difficulties, and here again your parson friend—the expert—will be of the greatest help. That there is a certain cruelty and hardness, a bigotry and insensitiveness to suffering, in some of the Old Testament tales cannot be denied, and you must on no account attempt to twist them or to hide this element from the children. But if they are wisely selected and told these splendid stories, apart from their own worth and the lessons they teach, do throw into magnificent relief the moral splendour of Jesus Christ.

Young children often find it difficult to grasp the difference between the Old Testament and the New—'Testament' is one of those difficult adult words of which I spoke in a previous chapter. Personally I should avoid the terms when dealing with very young children, classifying the stories instead into three groups—the 'Jesus' stories, the 'Before-Jesus' stories, and the 'After-Jesus' stories. "That was before Jesus came, you see" is a good enough answer, for the time being, to any criticisms the children may express about some of the saying and doings of Old Testament heroes. And of course your 'After-Jesus' stories—though you will find some grand examples in the Acts of the Apostles—will not be confined to the Bible. We have the whole splendid, even if sometimes tragic, history of the past two thousand years to draw upon, with its tales of the saints and heroes and common humble men and women (don't forget them) who have laboured and suffered nobly for the name, and in the power, of Jesus Christ. Use these stories freely; some of them may well be tales of men and women who are still alive and at work. They make an admirable foil to the Gospel stories—they *are* the Gospel stories, reproduced and re-lived in our midst. You will have to hunt for them, of course, and that will take time and trouble, but the very search for them will take you into regions of living experience and give you a new picture of the reality and power of religion which will be a possession to you for ever.

CHAPTER 9

THE GALILEE CHARTER

I have said little—some may think too little—so far in these pages about the devotional side of religion. I have approached the problem very largely from the standpoint of the fourth group of parents as they were classified in the fifth chapter, those who are ' starting from scratch ' without any very definite pre-conceptions about religion except a profound inward hunger—that sense of restlessness which Augustine tells us will never be satisfied till we find our rest in God. The steady effort, spread over many weeks and months, to study the Gospel story in detail and to re-create imaginatively its central figure can have but one effect upon any man or woman who approaches the task with real humility of mind; they will be filled with wonder, reverence, and a very lively curiosity. The wonder and the reverence may remain for a time unexpressed, working like a yeast in the deeper levels of the soul, but the curiosity must be satisfied somehow, and I shall be surprised if it does not drive the explorer to search in other parts of the New Testament, and in the pages of History, for further clues to that amazing character—Jesus of Nazareth. What are we to think of Him? Are we to take Him at his own valuation, or, if we reject it, what valuation are we to substitute? The Epistles and the Acts of the Apostles form a vivid and illuminating commentary on the life and work of Jesus; they are shot through with a sense of haste—almost of hurry—and yet underneath it all there lies the stillness of a great peace. Something had happened in time—just there it took place, and just then—but its significance is concerned with eternity. Paul's letters are full of this double content; he hurries from place to place with the restless energy of a commercial traveller seeking new markets, and yet underneath his restlessness there is a certainty which carries conviction to us as it did to his hearers in the Graeco-Roman world. The letters are intensely practical—almost business-letters sometimes—with their admonition, scolding, downright opinions, and advice about such matters as finance and diet, but he cannot scold for long—he is always breaking out into poetry, rising from his business-talk into a song of love and joy. And the theme is always the same, the eternal thing that has been done in the world of space and time, the eternal word that has been spoken to transitory man. " He lived for us ! " Paul cries as he hurries across the world attending to a thousand petty trifles; "He died for us ! He rose from the dead that we might share His conquest over all things ! I never saw Him in the flesh, but I have seen Him since—seen Him and heard Him and felt Him. He has laid hold of me and made me His own ; He is the answer to every question in heaven and earth, He is God's triumphant ' Yes ' to all the searchings of mankind ! " The fourth Gospel—that of St. John—makes difficult reading if you take it directly after the first three; it is full of strange philosophisings and obscure interpretations which are hard to grasp after the direct simplicity of the others. But if you read the Epistles and the Acts in between the difficulty disappears and you plunge into that tremendous first chapter as into a long-familiar pool. Of course ! That is what His friends had come to think of Him as the years went by and they saw Him under the aspect of eternity. And when we turn away from the Bible and search the records of the Christian Church throughout its two thousand years of history we find the same thing, the same sense of urgency overlying the sense of eternity, the same restlessness, the same love-songs, and the same stillness. You must study the best Christians, needless to say, if you are to find out the truth about Jesus just as you must study the best buildings if you are to apprehend the truth about architecture and the best paintings if you are to understand art. The existence of great art is not disproved by the crude daubs in a children's penny Comic, Lincoln Cathedral is not non-suited because of the rows of mean hovels in a Manchester slum, and Christianity is not de-bunked because there were salacious mediaeval priests or because the Inquisition was cruel or because one of the Chapel Deacons at Looting-on-the-Sly has just been convicted of embezzling the Sunday Missionary collection. If you want to understand Christianity and get a true insight into the nature of its Founder you must study it at its best, not at its worst, and if you do that you will find that the experience of the Apostles has been verified countless thousands of times throughout the years that divide them from our busy modern age of science. You will discover, as I have said, that the same two notes are sounded again and again in almost the same words, the note of haste—of urgency—and the note of eternal stillness. You will find this in the great leaders of the Church—Augustine, Bernard, Francis, Loyola, Ken, Temple, Studdart-Kennedy, Dick Shepherd—and you will find it too in many so-called heretics, in Bunyan and Fox and Wesley, in the Salvation Army and the Plymouth Brethren, and in scores of humble mission-rooms throughout the land. And the note, when it is genuine, is always a paraphrase of the language of Paul. " He lived for us ! He died for us ! He rose from the dead that we might share His conquest over all things ! I never saw Him in the flesh, but I have seen Him since—seen Him and heard Him and felt Him. He has laid hold of me and made me His own; He is the answer to every question in heaven and earth, He is God's triumphant ' Yes ' to all the searchings of mankind ! "

The late M. R. James in one of his ghost stories—magnificent examples of the story-telling art they are too, if you have strong nerves—tells a tale of an antiquary who, while pursuing innocently his researches into the family archives of an ancient Swedish house, suddenly finds to his horror that one of its antique owners has come alive under his touch and that a malignant and terrible spirit is following him relentlessly over land and ocean to destroy him. It is possible that some who embark on the family gang adventure in search of religion may undergo a somewhat parallel, though a very different, experience. They may discover that something is coming alive under their hand, that what they thought would be a biographical study in the cause of education is turning into an encounter with someone who is alive—and pursuing. What if the Apostles, after all, were right ? What if the Eternal really did, then and there, come into the world of matter and get mixed up with it in a new way, bringing into it a new kind of life ? Is it possible that eternity should have exhausted itself, become worn out, in a paltry two thousand years ? And if not—what are the implications ? Can we go on with this thing if we are in danger of finding that the Man we are reading about in a book is standing at our elbow making urgent demands upon us ? The adventure takes on a new aspect, it becomes more serious and we are disquieted. Perhaps it is going to take us further than we bargained for.

Even if these obstinate questionings do not present themselves immediately to the senior members of the family gang the expedition will not have proceeded for long before the whole united party is brought up against them. You will not be able to go very far with your stories about the deeds of Jesus of Nazareth before you find yourselves forced to take into account His words—His direct teaching. We are familiar with the ' Atlantic Charter ', a set of principles laid down to govern and direct political action; we shall soon find in the Gospels something which we may call, if you like, the ' Galilee Charter '. A great deal of it is contained in what is known as ' The Sermon on the Mount ' in the fifth, sixth, and seventh chapters of St. Matthew, but there are fragments of it embedded like jewels all through the Gospels. If you want a job for the older children to do you may find it a good idea to buy them two cheap copies of the New Testament (you will find that you need two for the purpose) and get them to cut out all the ' Charter ' passages and paste them into a book, ready for reference. One member of the crew—father might be a good man for the post—would be appointed as ' Keeper of the Charter ', and when the story is finished it may become a regular thing for somebody to ask him " Is there anything about that story in the Charter, Daddy ? " Suppose, for instance, that the story has been about the Prodigal son, in the fifteenth chapter of St. Luke. It deals, you remember, with the question of forgiveness—the amazing forgivingness of the injured father and the churlish un-forgivingness of the elder brother. When it is finished the

Keeper of the Charter will get to work, and it will not be long before he finds something very much to the point. "If ye forgive men their trespasses, your heavenly Father will also forgive you; but if ye forgive not men their trespasses, neither will your Father forgive your trespasses." He may possibly discover another passage, too, about leaving your gift before the altar and going off, before you present it to God, to be reconciled to the man who has a complaint against you. Well, that is straight enough in all conscience, and now you are up against it. I said earlier on that children are realists, and perhaps it will be Tommy who asks the question that puts the fat in the fire. "But, Daddy! When Mr. Smith cheated you over that bicycle last summer you said you'd never speak to him again—and you haven't!" "Yes, and you, Tommy" chimes in Betty, "When Tim Snooks stole those conkers out of your desk at school and smashed them all you said you'd never forgive him, and you know you hate him still!"

Yes, this is the crisis, and now you are up against it. Is this adventure of your family going to be just talk and pretty stories and playing with ideas, or are you going to take it seriously? This crisis is bound to come sooner or later, and you must be ready for it. What are you going to *do* about it? Is father, after puffing a while at his pipe in gloomy silence, going to say "Well, I've got to go round and see Smith tomorrow evening— that's all! I hate doing it, but I must—the Charter says so! And you, Tommy old man—what are you going to do about Tim Snooks? You'll have to do something, won't you?"

Yes, this is the acid test; this is the moment when the success or failure of your family adventure hangs in the balance. Those bitter estrangements, the sense of injury done or suffered, the long icy silences that make both forgiveness and atonement impossible—are they or are they not to go down before the Galilee Charter and the Man who made it? And there are other things besides forgiveness, as we shall find soon enough, for the teaching and the example of Jesus challenge our lives—and will challenge your gang—in a hundred ways. But it is the first crisis which counts most of all; if you laugh it off or put it aside or slur it over your expedition, however well begun, is doomed to wander aimlessly in the shallows and will soon peter out and be abandoned. But if you accept that first challenge and act upon it—then indeed you are launched upon perilous seas, for the Galilee Charter will have become alive in your family gang and the Man who made it will have joined your crew. To have Jesus Christ Himself in your family boat, taking the helm—that is real religion.

This is, I believe, for normal healthy-minded folk the right approach to that direct religious experience which stands revealed so clearly in the Epistles of Paul, in the fourth Gospel, and in the history of the Christian Church. The first step is imaginative apprehension through the stories, the second step is obedience, and the crowning gift is communion, but the communion—the direct personal experience—can only come through obedience. What is wrong with much 'popular' religion, particularly of the emotional type, is that it attempts to miss out or by-pass the obedience stage and to proceed straight from the apprehension to the communion. I would never dream of denying that this is a possible, or even a right, course for some people—there are a hundred different paths up the precipice to God and it would be worse than folly to attempt to close any one of them—but I do believe that for the majority of normal people, and certainly for the great majority of children, the obedience stage is a necessary tract that must be traversed between apprehension and communion. "If any man will do His will, he shall know of the doctrine" said Jesus, and He was well-versed in the psychology of children. Children learn through doing more quickly, and more thoroughly, than through any number of words, and though you may interest them and arrest their imaginations by the stories you tell about the Christ of Galilee He can never come really alive to them unless they see that His will is the law of the household, the guiding principle by which the senior members are seeking to direct their lives.

To attempt to stimulate the religious emotions of young children is indefensible, their emotions of love and trust are, or ought to be, wholly centred in the family circle and are not yet capable of being either generalised or extended to someone they have never seen and never met. I would, myself, no more dream of telling a young child that he should 'love' Jesus than I would tell him that he should 'love' his third cousin Archibald who lives in Australia and whom he has never seen. The children must see Jesus and meet with Him before they can love Him; you may help them to see Him through the imaginative power of your stories, but they can only meet Him through obedience, through the coming alive of the Galilee Charter within the circle of the family gang. Neither children nor grown-ups can fall in love to order, they can only do it through acquaintance.

I have spoken of the 'obedience stage' in terms which might suggest, possibly, that it is an easy matter to apply the Galilee Charter to the every-day affairs of family life. Nothing, of course, could be further from the truth; it is the hardest thing in the world to 'do His will'—so hard that any man or family that makes the attempt, however seriously and strenuously, must inevitably be far more conscious of failure than of success. It is not only the conventions of the world that make obedience difficult, we find out soon enough that the main resistance lies within ourselves. We are not alone in this experience, right at the beginning of things Paul himself—to turn back to the Epistles—was only too bitterly aware of that fatal gap that lies between willing and doing, between the knowledge of good and the power to obey. In the seventh chapter of Romans he lays bare to us, with that matchless power of burning eloquence of which he was a master, the terrible conflict which was tearing his very soul to pieces. He drags back the curtain from his innermost life and writhes before us in torment, and even as we watch his agony we know well enough that he is but staging the drama of our own personal experience. "What I would," he cries, "that I do not; but what I hate, that I do" and again—"to will is present with me; but how to perform that which is good I find not. For the good that I would, I do not; but the evil which I would not, that I do. I find then a law, that, when I would do good, evil is present with me. For I delight in the law of God after the inward man: but I see another law in my members, warring against the law of my mind, and bringing me into captivity to the law of sin which is in my members." And he finishes with a cry that has found its echo in the minds of countless thousands who, since his day, have tried to mould their conduct to the pattern of the Galilee Charter. "Wretch that I am!" he exclaims, "Who shall deliver me from this corpse to which I am chained?"

That is the bitter experience, the valley of agony and humiliation, through which every man and woman must pass who makes the attempt to follow Jesus of Nazareth. There is no escape from it, it is a tempest inevitable to the seas through which your family boat is setting its course, and you must be prepared for it. The children will not realise it, of course,—not yet—but *you* will have to go through it, and it will drive you to your knees. There is no other thing to be done, you cannot go on with this business without prayer. The apprehension through the Gospel stories is, after all, so imperfect; the picture is so shadowy, so blurred—and how do you know that it is not, after all, just a creation of your own imagination? And the obedience, the attempt to carry out the Galilee Charter within the family life and outside, is such a ludicrous failure. The good that you love you do not, and the evil that you hate—that is what gets done, after all. Something more is needed, something for *you*, the senior members, first, and then for the whole family gang. It is not enough to make mental pictures of Jesus and then to try to do His will, you must speak to Him, and He must speak to you.

The family gang must learn to pray.

CHAPTER X.

THE GANG AT PRAYER

And so we come to prayer, the crown of the whole adventure. To those parents who were brought up in religious homes it may seem a natural and easy step for the family gang to turn from the fascination of the story and from the discussion of the Charter to the simple act of prayer, but to others who are approaching the adventure from a more agnostic standpoint it may well be a step of almost impossible difficulty. Something fundamental is involved in the step, something that concerns their very sanity itself. Many of us have pretended, when we were amusing the children, to hold a conversation down a dead telephone with someone who was not there, but to do such a thing seriously, not as a game but in deadly earnest, savours of madness. It may be that some who read these words may feel that their intellectual integrity is involved in this matter, that to institute prayer as a part of their family adventure would be to compromise their honour. To such I can only say that honour must come first, under no circumstances must sincerity be sacrificed to expediency either in the secret inner life of the individual or in the community of the family gang. But I would beg them also to consider deeply and critically the reasons—perhaps the emotions—which appear to make prayer impossible to them. Are you quite sure that the fundamental reasons are not pride, or fear, or both? Neither pride nor fear are 'respectable' feelings, they belong to that type of emotion to which I referred in the first section of this book, the type that is not accepted by the censor enthroned at the threshold of our conscious mind and is therefore turned back and not re-admitted till it has camouflaged itself under some more acceptable guise. Both pride and fear are adepts at the art of camouflage, and intellectual honesty is a favourite—and a most successful—disguise for them. The little boy tiptoes along the dark passage on the top floor and lays his hand, hesitatingly, on the door-handle of an equally dark room. Then his heart fails him and he scurries down the stairs into the light and warmth of the lower regions. " I didn't go in " he assures himself " because I knew there wasn't anybody inside ! " That is reasonable, his intellectual integrity is satisfied, but the *truth* is that he did not enter because he was afraid there *might* be some one—or something—there, not because he knew there wasn't. So it is with prayer; many of us refuse to pray, not because we are sure that there is nobody to hear, but because we are afraid that there *may* be some one. A great deal of what we fondly imagine to be our intellectual honesty is really fear wearing one of his fancy dresses.

Pride is an even more potent enemy of prayer than fear, and one equally good at the art of deception. It is not an accident that men have formed the habit of kneeling when they pray, for prayer is the most humiliating exercise that man can undertake. We are not humiliated because God is a splendid King, throned in dazzling magnificence amid a host of flaming cherubim. Men used to think like that about God—projecting upon Him their own childish ideal of grandeur—but we cannot, or should not, so think of Him when once we have caught sight of Jesus of Nazareth. It is not the grandeur of God that drives us Christians to our knees, it is His utter humility. Grandeur we might have withstood—who are we that we should truckle to magnificence ?—but humility is irresistible, we cannot stand against it. If God had been proud, as we are proud, our tiny pride might have raised itself against His, pitifully defending the citadel of our being against His challenge, but how can we defend ourselves against His humility, what barriers can we raise against His compassion ? Our pride withers away before it and we fall upon our knees—not because we are humble and God is great but because we thought we were great and we find that God is humble. For when He came to show Himself to us He was born in a shed at the back of an inn-yard, He worked at a tradesman's bench and spoke with a rustic accent, He tramped the roads a penniless vagrant, destitute of possessions, He let Himself be bound hand

and foot and allowed men to spit in His face unrebuked, and He died on a felon's gallows. Jesus broke to pieces, once and for ever, man's mistaken ideas about the splendour of God; these ideas were primitive, born from the pageant of oriental despotism and decked with all its trappings of arbitrary power. But just because they are primitive these ideas die hard in us; you have only to turn over the pages of any Christian hymn-book to see how they have crept back, in spite of the revelation of Jesus, into Christian thought. Yes, Christ was humble—we cannot deny that—but surely it was a temporary gesture only, surely God, after He had stepped down from His Sapphire Throne to visit us, re-ascended it again in splendour ? Surely our pride must have some counterpart in Him ? So we argue, because thrones are in our blood, they are part of our essential nature, however democratic we may be in politics. We all occupy a throne, we all sit aloof in fancied power within the citadel of our own ego, we all want to be monarchs of our own innermost being and we cannot get it out of our heads that God must want to sit on the throne of the universe. But He doesn't, and that is the message which Jesus brought to mankind—and which mankind refused to receive. God has never sat on a throne, has never wanted to, and never will. He has never worn a crown—except a crown of thorns—and He never will. He has never been proud, and He never will be. He has never been in a palace, He has never been anywhere else than in a stable, or at a carpenter's bench, or on the road, or on the gallows—and He never will be. Jesus does not reveal a gesture of God, He reveals His nature; and that does not change, it is eternal. That is the meaning of the Eternal Christ.

If the humility of God drives us to our knees His compassion sends us upon our faces in the dust. Of all the words to which the New Testament has given new life and meaning perhaps 'compassion' is the greatest. It means pity, but more than pity; it means sympathy, but more than sympathy; it means love and gentleness, but it means strength too, and it is not without a hint of anger—that strange, selfless anger, utterly free from pride, with which Jesus met and shrivelled the scorn of the Pharisees.

Above all it means action, for compassion is a thing of the will and the muscles as much as of the heart; it is love in action, it is redemption. If God had been humility alone we might, in the blindness of our pride, have turned from Him in scorn, but against humility and compassion united we have no defence.

I have written of these things at some length because it is important, if we are to learn to pray, that we should understand what—or Who—is at the other end of our prayer. But what is at this end ? The humiliation of prayer does not arise only from our apprehension of what stands at the other end of it—the humility and compassion of God—but from what stands at our end of it, the fortified citadel of our own soul. The use of this word 'citadel' is no idle metaphor, it is one of the basic facts of human psychology. Life is a 'principle of individuation' and right from our birth it is our main, absorbing task to nourish and increase our individuality and to protect it from the assaults of the outside world. So from the beginning we set to work upon the fortifications that are to divide us off from the rest of the universe, the stockade that is to enclose that tiny plot we call our 'self', in which we can reign in undisputed possession. We guard the gateway jealously, repelling all invaders and admitting only that which will add to the dignity and the self-esteem of him who sits upon the throne within. We are very sensitive about the prestige of that inner ruler so we decorate our fortifications, on their outer side, with a façade of advertisement to proclaim to the outer world the nature of that which we like to think is reigning within. Some people live all their lives in the outer perimeter of their souls, trafficking busily with the world, throwing their weight about, impressing themselves on other people. They are conscious only of the outside surface of their walls, they spend their lives touching up and enhancing the advertisements that hang there to impress the world; but they never go inside, the citadel is deserted, they do not know what manner of man they are—they have never been inside to see. We call them extroverts. Others live at the opposite extreme; through some childish experience of frustration or inferiority, accepted deep into their unconscious mind, they face their outer walls with plates of impenetrable steel and retire into the citadel, alone, where they live a life of dream and phantasy. They are not concerned to impress the world or to advertise their wares, they only want to be left alone. Theirs is the bitterest of all prides, the pride of shame. They crouch on the pitiful throne of selfhood, clutching the tinsel crown and the tawdry sceptre, keeping the world at a distance because they know—or think they know—with what scorn the world would assess their kingship and assay their tinsel. And sometimes—such is the mystery of life—out of their dreams they produce poetry or music or art that shakes the world, dazzling mankind with the vision of eternal beauty. We call these people introverts; they suffer more than other people and they always have to suffer alone. Perhaps that is why God has such compassion for them; perhaps that is why He gives them, sometimes, the gift of poetry and the secret ecstatic joy of beauty.

But whether we are extroverts or introverts—or, as is much more usual, a fantastic mixture of the two—we are all alike in our secret passion for self-kingship and in the possession of those fortifications with which we seek to defend it.

That is what is sitting at the hither end of the telephone of prayer; a king crouching on his throne behind fortifications of steel, guarding his tiny kingdom with a fanatical tenacity that is rooted in the most primary instinct of life, the instinct of self-preservation. That is why prayer is so desperately hard, so shatteringly humiliating. For prayer is nothing less that the letting down of the drawbridge, the breaching of the walls, the surrender of the very citadel of life. It violates the deepest instinct we possess, the instinct for personal kingship; that is what Paul meant, I think, when he said that we must be crucified with Christ, for real prayer is crucifixion—it is the abdication of kingship. It is not what we let out when we pray that humiliates us, it is what we let in. You cannot conduct the traffic of prayer in a one-way street, if your prayer is no more than petition, praise, or confession it may be but oratory. What matters in prayer is not what we let out but what we let in; it is not lowering the drawbridge to despatch an embassy to an outside power—even if that power be God—it is lowering the drawbridge and breaching the walls that some one may come in. And He who waits without, so patient in the dust, is not a mighty King whom we can welcome to the citadel while we wear our crown and hold the sceptre in our hand, He comes as a carpenter wearing a threadbare coat, His face is covered with dust and sweat (yes, sweat as it were great drops of blood), He speaks with a peasant's burr, and His hands are so maimed that you cannot bear to look at them. The crown and the sceptre of our individual pride are out of place with such a guest; our trouble is not that we have not a fair enough garment wherewith to deck ourselves when we admit the King of Kings, but that we have not a coat old or patched or cheap enough to match with His. It is not good manners to put on your best suit when you entertain a penniless beggar at your table. Prayer is the deepest personal humilation, it is the admission of humility and compassion to the throne of your inmost self, it is the surrender of your cherished citadel to a Man with a cheap coat and torn hands. The hardest thing about prayer is that it kills pride.

All that I have written so far in this chapter concerns the adult members of the crew, not the children, but it is only right that we parents should know the ultimate implications of prayer before we attempt to introduce it as part of the daily practice of the family gang adventure. There is no need for the children to become extroverts or introverts, or even that uneasy mixture of the two which is the cause of so much inner conflict to so many. To the adult who approaches prayer late in life, when his defences have long been embattled with the granite of prejudice, the act of surrender may indeed be a process of crucifixion, but it need not be so with a child. The admission of humility and compassion to the citadel is not an unnatural act, contrary to the course of evolution, it is the best possible assurance that the growth of the individual being should be healthy, free, and unrepressed. Prayer—provided that it is genuine two-way prayer and not mere oratory—is the best possible corrective to both introversion and extroversion, and the children cannot begin it too young. Children understand compassion more instinctively than do the majority of adults and they are less obsessed with the differences between carpenters and kings; however much they may at times appear to strut and brag the humility of the carpenter is more natural to them than it is to us. "Whosoever therefore shall humble himself as this little child, the same is greatest in the Kingdom of Heaven" was a remark directed to an adult audience, not to the children.

Your aim, then, in your family gang prayers will be to lead the children into touch with the source of humility and compassion, and when they find Him He will not be so strange a figure to them, I fancy, as He was to you. Just how the practice of prayer is to be introduced to them is a matter which depends so much on the spirit of the particular family, and on the traditions and training of the senior members, that I hesitate to do more than throw out a few suggestions. But I do suggest that prayer, since religion began as a communal affair, should first be introduced as a 'gang' activity—something the family do together as a united effort—rather than as an individual act. Individual prayer should, I think, grow out of communal prayer. When the story and the Charter-discussion are over, let the family kneel down together—round the table or by one of the children's beds—and speak for a few moments with the Steersman of their crew. I know of one small family of three, where the boy is a Rugby football enthusiast, in which this family prayer is known as the 'scrum'; they kneel down together by the bed, arms interlocked in the approved Rugby fashion, and the junior chooses which of the seniors is to 'put the ball in,' as he calls it. There must be some silence, of course, while you think about the Carpenter and realise His presence, and then perhaps one of the seniors will offer to Him, in the name of the gang, the loyalty and obedience of all, with special reference to any point which has come out of the story or the Charter, praying Him that He will give something of His compassion and His humility to this particular group of His friends. Then you may say together the family prayer of all

Christians—the best of all gang prayers—very slowly and reverently, on no account to be gabbled through as a piece of routine. You may, in addition, care to use some of the great prayers of the Church—that will depend a good deal on the nature of the particular convoy with which you have cast in your lot. But keep it alive, and do not let it drop into mere routine. In many ways children like routine, as do their elders; it saves trouble and gives a sense of familiarity and continuity which is by no means to be despised. We have to steer a middle course, as we have to do so often in this business of education, between two extremes. If there is no routine the result will be instability and even anarchy, the habit of prayer will never be formed—and the formation of good habits is vital to the children's growth; on the other hand routine is deadening, and we must never allow the children—or ourselves—to get the idea that saying a prayer is the same thing as praying. This is just one of the many sandbanks we shall encounter on our voyage.

You must watch carefully for the moment when, for each child in turn, the gang prayer is to be supplemented by the individual act. If the Guest of compassion and humility has been admitted, and welcomed, into the citadel of the family gang the time must come when each member of it will realise that there is another door yet to be opened, the gateway of the individual keep. This step should never be forced upon a child—some are ready for it sooner and some later—but it may be encouraged when the time seems ripe for it. Just how the opportunity for private prayer is to be arranged will vary from family to family, but it will be the seniors' job to see that the opportunity is provided when it is needed and the due encouragement given. One possible arrangement would be for the family 'scrum'—the united gang prayer —to take place at night when the children are going to bed and for each individual member of the gang to have his own private time of prayer—if he wants it—when he gets up in the morning. Sixty generations of Christians have found by experience that the 'morning watch' is well worth keeping, even at a little cost to personal comfort.

Finally, should we make the children say their prayers, or should it be voluntary ? In spite of the argument for habit-formation to which I have just referred I would urge, myself, the voluntary principle. Neither the stories nor the Charter nor the prayers should be forced upon the children against their will—that is one reason why the stories must be well told, they must be sufficiently attractive to attract. But it may well be that the children will not want a story every night or, having had a story, want a ' scrum.' Very well : do not force it on them ; " Father and I will have our prayer alone to-night when we go to bed " you can say. But mind you do have it—you must keep your word.

I have said very little about dogma and doctrine in these pages. That is not because I regard these as being unimportant—indeed they are a vital factor in adult religion—but because I do not myself regard them as being the main concern of family religion in the home. I would suggest that you leave them aside, as it were, until the children begin to ask questions about them on their own account. Then you must answer, as best you can, in terms of your own belief, with the guidance and help of your Church if you belong to one—as I hope you will. But the answers must be your *belief* and you must not be afraid to reply " I am not quite sure about that—I haven't thought it out yet " if that is the true state of affairs. If these things are not real to you they will not become real to the children through a merely conventional answer.

This, then, is the threefold aim of the family gang adventure in search of God : firstly to make, through the medium of stories, Jesus of Nazareth and the whole drama of religion through the ages come vividly alive to the children ; secondly to make the way of life revealed by those stories and by the Galilee Charter—the way of humility and compassion—the rule of life for the family ; thirdly to discover, individually and corporately, the meaning and the practice of prayer. The adventure, if pursued faithfully, will lead you inevitably to ally yourself with a Church, if you do not belong to one already, for it is no more possible to be a real Christian without belonging to a Church than it is to be a real soldier without belonging to an army. Real religion, though it makes its ultimate demand on the inner citadel of every individual soul, began as a communal instinct and only in the wider community can it find its complete fulfilment. To many, who already belong to such a community, this will be a self-evident truth, and from the beginning they will conduct their family expedition within its fellowship. Others, who are starting as it were from scratch, may have to search for their true spiritual home with doubts and misgivings, but in the end they must find it if they are to understand the true significance of humility and compassion in human life.

Heaven-on-Thames—the ideal society for which we strive—must be founded on humility and compassion if the kingdoms of this world are to become the kingdoms of our Lord and of His Christ. There is no other basis on which individual, family, or civic life can be founded if it is to be true to the line of evolution, in harmony with the long and patient purposes of God. And Heaven-on-Thames can only be kept free from pride—that deadliest of the seven deadly sins, that curse of society, that devil-sire of war and cruelty and exploitation—if it is built up of families which have opened their doors and their hearts to the Lord of humility and compassion. For the family gang is the womb of both the individual and the state, it is the one primary group from which all our human equipment, of body and mind, is derived, the one natural society through which the rule of humility and compassion can enter as a living force into the world of men, binding together the new brain and the old, the past and the present, intellect and instinct, into the pattern which God intends.

Heaven-on-Thames will come at last when every family gang is named after the Carpenter with the worn coat and the maimed hands and feet, the Lord of humility and compassion, the same yesterday, and to-day, and for ever.

For Product Safety Concerns and Information please contact our EU
representative GPSR@taylorandfrancis.com
Taylor & Francis Verlag GmbH, Kaufingerstraße 24, 80331 München, Germany

www.ingramcontent.com/pod-product-compliance
Lightning Source LLC
Chambersburg PA
CBHW052134300426
44116CB00010B/1899